CONDUCTING
ACTION
RESEARCH

for BUSINESS and MANAGEMENT STUDENTS

WITHDRAWN

Sara Miller McCune founded SAGE Publishing in 1965 to support the dissemination of usable knowledge and educate a global community. SAGE publishes more than 1000 journals and over 800 new books each year, spanning a wide range of subject areas. Our growing selection of library products includes archives, data, case studies and video. SAGE remains majority owned by our founder and after her lifetime will become owned by a charitable trust that secures the company's continued independence.

Los Angeles | London | New Delhi | Singapore | Washington DC | Melbourne

CONDUCTING ACTION RESEARCH

for BUSINESS and MANAGEMENT STUDENTS

DAVID COGHLAN & ABRAHAM B. (RAMI) SHANI

Los Angeles | London | New Delhi
Singapore | Washington DC | Melbourne

Los Angeles | London | New Delhi
Singapore | Washington DC

SAGE Publications Ltd
1 Oliver's Yard
55 City Road
London EC1Y 1SP

SAGE Publications Inc.
2455 Teller Road
Thousand Oaks, California 91320

SAGE Publications India Pvt Ltd
B 1/I 1 Mohan Cooperative Industrial Area
Mathura Road
New Delhi 110 044

SAGE Publications Asia-Pacific Pte Ltd
3 Church Street
#10-04 Samsung Hub
Singapore 049483

Editor: Kirsty Smy
Editorial assistant: Lyndsay Aitken
Production editor: Martin Fox
Copyeditor: Christine Bitten
Proofreader: Sharon Cawood
Marketing manager: Alison Borg
Cover design: Franics Kenney
Typeset by: C&M Digitals (P) Ltd, Chennai, India
Printed in the UK

Library of Congress Control Number: 2018930686

British Library Cataloguing in Publication data

A catalogue record for this book is available from the
British Library

ISBN 978-1-5264-0477-0
ISBN 978-1-5264-0478-7 (pbk)

At SAGE we take sustainability seriously. Most of our products are printed in the UK using responsibly
sourced papers and boards. When we print overseas we ensure sustainable papers are used as
measured by the PREPS grading system. We undertake an annual audit to monitor our sustainability.

CONTENTS

EDITORS' INTRODUCTION TO THE *MASTERING BUSINESS RESEARCH METHODS* SERIES

Welcome to the *Mastering Business Research Methods* series. In recent years, there has been a great increase in the numbers of students reading for Masters-level degrees across the business and management disciplines. A considerable number of these students are expected to prepare a dissertation towards the end of their degree programme in a time frame of three to four months. For many students, this takes place after their taught modules have finished and is expected to be an independent piece of work. Whilst each student is supported in his or her dissertation or research project by an academic supervisor, s/he will need to find out more detailed information about the method that s/he intends to use. Before starting dissertations or research projects, students have usually been provided with little more than an overview in a wide range of methods in preparation for what is often a daunting task. If you are one such student, you are not alone. As university professors with a deep interest in research methods, we have provided this series of books to help people like you. Each book provides detailed information about a particular method, approach or task to support you in your dissertation. We understand both what is involved in Masters-level dissertations and what help students need to understand research methods in order to excel when writing a dissertation. This series is the only one that is designed with the specific objective of helping Masters-level students to prepare their dissertations.

Most books in our series are dedicated to either a method of data collection or a method of data analysis. Those books are intended to be read by you when undertaking the particular stage of the research process – of either data collection or analysis – and they are designed to provide sufficient knowledge to complete that stage. There are some other books, such as the book about *Action Research*, where the nature of the approach means that one method is inextricably linked with others. Such books are designed to provide you with a comprehensive understanding of the approach, although it may be necessary to supplement your reading of one or other of these books by reading another book on a particular method that you intend to employ when utilizing that approach. All books in the series are written in a clear way by highly respected authors who have considerable experience of teaching and writing about research methods. To help you find your way around each book, we have utilized a standard format. That is to say that each book is organized into six chapters:

- **Chapter 1** introduces the method, considers how the method emerged for what purposes, and provides an outline of the remainder of the book.
- **Chapter 2** addresses the underlying philosophical assumptions that inform the uses of particular methods.
- **Chapter 3** discusses the components of the relevant method.
- **Chapter 4** considers the way in which the different components may be organized to use the method.
- **Chapter 5** provides examples of published studies that have used the method.
- **Chapter 6** concludes by reflecting on the strengths and weaknesses of that method.

We hope that reading your chosen books helps you in your dissertation.

Bill Lee, Mark N.K. Saunders and Vadake K. Narayanan

ABOUT THE SERIES EDITORS

Bill Lee, PhD is Professor of Accounting at the University of Sheffield, UK. He has a long-standing interest in research methods and practice, in addition to his research into accounting and accountability issues. Bill's research has been published widely, including in: *Accounting Forum*; *British Accounting Review*; *Critical Perspectives on Accounting*; *Journal of Applied Behavioral Science*; *Management Accounting Research*; *Omega*; *Organization Studies* and *Work, Employment & Society*. His publications in the area of research methods and practice include the co-edited collections *The Real Life Guide to Accounting Research* and *Challenges and Controversies in Management Research*.

Mark N.K. Saunders, BA MSc PGCE PhD FCIPD is Professor of Business Research Methods and Director of PhD Programmes at Birmingham Business School, University of Birmingham, UK. His research interests are research methods, in particular methods for participant selection and for understanding intra-organizational relationships; human resource aspects of the management of change, in particular trust within and between organizations; and small and medium-sized enterprises. Mark's research has been published in journals including *British Journal of Management*, *Journal of Small Business Management*, *Field Methods*, *Human Relations*, *Management Learning* and *R&D Management*, *Social Science and Medicine*. He has co-authored and co-edited a range of books, including *Research Methods for Business Students* (currently in its 7th edition) and the *Handbook of Research Methods on Trust* (currently in its 2nd edition).

Vadake K. Narayanan is the Deloitte Touché Stubbs Professor of Strategy and Entrepreneurship in Le Bow College of Business, Drexel University, Philadelphia, PA. His articles have appeared in leading professional journals such as *Academy of Management Journal*, *Academy of Management Review*, *Accounting Organizations and Society*, *Journal of Applied Psychology*, *Journal of Management*, *Journal of Management Studies*, *Management Information Systems Quarterly*, *R&D Management* and *Strategic Management Journal*. He has authored or co-authored several books, including *Managing Technology and Innovation for Competitive Advantage* (Pearson), and has co-edited the *Encyclopaedia of Technology and Innovation Management* (Wiley).

ABOUT THE AUTHORS

David Coghlan is Professor Emeritus and Fellow Emeritus at the Trinity Business School, University of Dublin, Trinity College Dublin, Ireland. He specializes in organization development and action research and is active in both communities internationally. He has published over 160 articles and book chapters. His book, *Doing Action Research in Your Own Organization* (SAGE) has been through four editions with a fifth one in progress. He is co-editor of the *SAGE Encyclopedia of Action Research* (2014). Recent co-authored books include *Collaborative Strategic Improvement through Network Action Learning* (Edward Elgar, 2011) and *Organizational Change and Strategy* (2nd edn, Routledge, 2016). He is currently on the editorial boards of: *Journal of Applied Behavioral Science*, *Action Research*, *Action Learning: Research and Practice*, *Systemic Practice and Action Research* and *The OD Practitioner*, among others.

Abraham B. (Rami) Shani is Professor of Management at the Orfalea College of Business, California Polytechnic University and Visiting International Professor at the School of Management, Politecnico di Milano, Milan, Italy. His research interests include organizational change and development, collaborative research methodologies, learning in and by organizations, sustainability and sustainable effectiveness. Rami is author, co-author or co-editor of 33 books and over 160 articles and chapters. He is co-editor of *The Handbook of Collaborative Management Research* (SAGE, 2008) and of the annual series, *Research in Organization Change and Development*, volumes 17–26 (Emerald, 2008–2018). He and David Coghlan have co-edited *The Fundamentals of Organization Development* (4 volumes, SAGE, 2010) and *Action Research in Business and Management* (4 volumes, SAGE, 2014). He serves on the editorial board of five journals.

LIST OF FIGURES AND TABLES

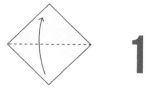

1

INTRODUCING ACTION RESEARCH

INTRODUCTION

This chapter introduces action research as a research approach, which aims at both taking action and creating knowledge together. It is practised in all fields of social action including organization development, business and management, education, nursing and health care, social work and community development. Within business and management, as Coghlan and Shani (2016) demonstrate, it is practised across multiple sectors and business disciplines. It is found in industries, such as banking, mining, automotive, healthcare, electronics, pharmaceutical, food, manufacturing, energy and media, and is practised in business disciplines, such as general management, operations management, marketing, information technology, accounting, finance, e-commerce and human resources.

Action research is a commonly adopted approach in masters programmes where the students may be experienced practitioners and are engaging in their programmes in a part-time capacity and have expectations that the output from their programmes will be directly useful to their organizations. Action research is also viewed as a managerial approach to taking action and while doing so embedding in the practice a scientific discovery process that can enhance both the action and generate a deeper level understanding of the issue at hand. Action research is ideally placed to meet both requirements of an academic programme and organizational usefulness. Where the students are not experienced practitioners and are not attached to an organizational system, they typically work under the close direction of a supervisor who is overseeing an organizational intervention. They may be part of a wider research project where there is a team of researchers and any single masters dissertation is a concurrent contribution to the larger project.

This chapter is structured as follows. First, we introduce the foundations of action research, providing a definition which will form the basis of the book and locating it in the work of Kurt Lewin, in forms of knowledge production and in dialogic organization development. Second, we describe the origins of action research and locate it in the philosophy of Aristotle, the social psychology of Kurt Lewin in organization development, in sociotechnical systems and design thinking. Third, we introduce how action research works through cycles of action. Finally, we introduce the distinction between a *core* project and a *dissertation* project as central to those engaging in action research as a masters dissertation.

Throughout this and other chapters we invite you to pause and apply the theoretical points of the chapter to your dissertation project. We do this by means of 'Questions for Reflection'. Here we pose questions and invite you to answer them for yourself in reflections in a reflective journal which we introduce later in this chapter. These reflections are aimed at capturing your insights as you consider your action research project and at enabling you to plan how you will work and with whom in an action research mode. The questions are not comprehensive nor are they a school exercise to be completed. You may think of other questions that are worth considering and we encourage you to pursue those too. Accordingly, the reflections from these 'Questions for Reflection' show your work in progress. Later, as your work develops, you will verify some insights and discard others as you replace them with new insights from your experience.

WHAT IS ACTION RESEARCH?

As the term suggests, action research integrates both action and research, unlike traditional research approaches which focus on knowledge creation only. Accordingly, the distinction between data collection and data analysis of other research traditions does not apply as in action research they are inextricably linked.

Box 1.1 introduces the story of Kevin, a part-time MBA student, and illustrates how he took the opportunity confronting him as a manager to select/choose/define his dissertation topic. We will follow Kevin's story through these opening chapters and provide a further extended example in Chapter 4.

Box 1.1   Finding your action research project

Kevin found the lecture on insider action research in his part-time MBA research methods course very revealing and stimulating. He had been struggling with the task of finding a dissertation topic as he found the notion of research as he understood it to be somewhat removed from his concerns as a manager. In this lecture he was exposed to an approach to research that was grounded in the notion of researching in action and that he could engage in as an insider member of his own organization. He had some challenging issues ahead in his managerial role and the prospect of combining tackling them with doing his MBA dissertation appeared to offer him an opportunity to use his actual experience in his organization and be of practical use both to himself in completing his MBA and to his organization. His firm had recently been acquired by a larger firm and the acquisition meant that his section would now comprise members of the former acquiring organization as well as his own former colleagues of the acquired organization. Kevin had retained his position as section head and was responsible for the integration of the two groups into the section. The acquiring company was moving into Kevin's building. Kevin knew that there was a good deal of anxiety among his staff about the new organization and the arrival of new colleagues. The talk among his own former staff was that they were anxious about losing the work atmosphere that they valued and they feared being dominated by the incoming group, which, after all, was the acquiring company. His new staff would be arriving in two weeks' time. From the MBA modules on mergers and acquisitions and managing change, Kevin knew that his situation was pretty typical and that unless he managed the process of integration, it could be a disaster. He decided to adopt the preparation of his team for the arrival management of new members as the topic for his MBA dissertation.

Questions for Reflection

Does Kevin's situation and his sense of the opportunity to combine his forthcoming managerial challenge with his MBA dissertation evoke ideas for you as you consider a topic for your dissertation? Is there an existing or upcoming organizational challenge that is on your desk – or perhaps the desk of a friend or relative – which could form the foundation of an action research dissertation? Did one of your colleagues consult you or share with you a challenge that she was facing that might be an interesting possible topic to explore? Write a reflection on your provisional answers to these questions in your reflective journal.

Definition of Action Research

Drawing on an earlier definition by Shani and Pasmore (2016: 191) the definition of action research that we are following in this book is:

> An emergent inquiry process in which applied behavioural science knowledge is integrated with existing organizational knowledge and applied to address real organizational issues. It is simultaneously concerned with bringing about change in organizations, in developing self-help competencies in organizational members and in adding to scientific knowledge. Finally it is an evolving process that is undertaken in a spirit of collaboration and co-inquiry.

This definition captures the critical themes of the approach that constitute action research: that as an *emergent inquiry process* it engages in an unfolding story, where data shift as a consequence of intervention and where it is not possible to predict or to control what takes place with a high degree of accuracy. As an emergent process, action research involves researching in the present tense as Chandler and Torbert (2003) and Coghlan and Shani (2017) elaborate. Much of what we refer to as qualitative research is focused on the past. Action research builds on the past and takes place in the present with a view to shaping the future. It focuses on *real organizational issues*, rather than issues created particularly for the purposes of research. It operates in the domain of how people participate in systems and so *applied behavioural science knowledge* (i.e. the range of disciplines such as organizational psychology, organization theory, management, team working and so on) is both engaged in and drawn upon. Action research's distinctive characteristic is that it addresses the twin tasks of bringing about *change in organizations* and in generating robust, actionable *knowledge*, in an evolving process that is undertaken in a spirit of *collaboration and co-inquiry*, whereby research is constructed *with* people, rather than *on* or *for* them.

A Complete Theory of Action Research

Shani and Pasmore (2016) present a comprehensive theory of the action research process in terms of four factors (see Figure 1.1).

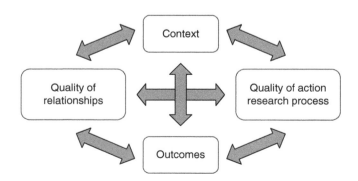

Figure 1.1   Complete theory of action research

- *Context*: These factors set the context of the action research project. Environmental factors in the global and local economies provide the larger context in which action research takes place. The more local context of organizational characteristics, such as resources, history, formal and informal organizations and the degrees of congruence between them, affects the readiness and capability for participating in action research. Individual goals may differ and impact the direction of the project, while shared goals enhance collaboration. Mapping out the context in as comprehensive a way as possible is critical.
- *Quality of relationships*: The quality of relationships between members of the system and researchers is paramount and evolves during the action research process. Hence the relationships need to be designed for and managed through shared goals, collaborative action, trust building, developing a common language, shared reflection and so on.
- *Quality of the action research process itself*: The quality of the emerging action research process is grounded in the dual focus on both the inquiry process and the implementation process. As the dual intent is to trigger action and generate new insights, paying attention to 'how' the project is progressing through continuous collaborative cycles is essential.
- *Outcomes*: The dual outcomes of action research are a) improved organizational practice and the development of self-help competencies and b) the creation of actionable theory through the action and inquiry. The added value to the organization is critical for the research to be permitted and, as such, the outcomes are viewed as enhanced systems of practice and knowledge that impact human, economic and ecological sustainability.

To return to Kevin's story we can see the four factors operative in his dissertation project.

Box 1.2   The four factors

The practical business and managerial context of Kevin's dissertation work lay in the acquisition of his firm by another firm and the need to make this acquisition work. The academic context told him that mergers and acquisitions typically do not work effectively because of a failure to address issues relating to cultural integration. Kevin foresaw several challenges. In order to build a new integrated section team he would have to create a climate of openness in his team and facilitate a shared preparation for its members to be open and welcoming of the upcoming new situation. He also needed to attend to the academic process of reading relevant literatures on mergers and acquisitions and on team development and show how this reading informed his actions in enabling integration to take place.

Questions for Reflection

How does Kevin's understanding of his situation and his projected action research project inform your thinking? What are the salient challenges from the external and internal environments that are creating the imperative for your action research project? Who are the key people with whom you need to collaborate? How might you design their engagement in the proposed action and knowledge generation? How might you develop the partnership? What might be some of the possible roadblocks in the study of the challenge? What are your hoped-for outcomes, both for the firm and for the knowledge you generate? Write a reflection on your provisional answers to these questions in your reflective journal.

THE ORIGINS OF ACTION RESEARCH

Action research integrates knowledge creation and practice through a collaborative process. Through clarifying the philosophical and historical foundations of the separation between knowledge and practice and more recent calls for integration, we can better mark the way forward towards a more balanced approach that addresses both basic knowledge and practice. In this section we trace the origins of different philosophies of science in Aristotle's writings. We illustrate by characterizing how, through action research and similar paradigms, the re-emergence of Aristotle's second, less celebrated legacy offers a significant opportunity for management practice.

Aristotle's Legacies and Philosophies of Science

Interestingly, both the legacy of separating theory and practice and subsequent calls for their integration emanate from Aristotle's work more than 2000 years ago. Inspired by his mentors Plato and Socrates, Aristotle initially distinguished the spheres of scientific knowledge, and of craft and experience, as two separate domains in Book VI of the *Nicomachean Ethics* (Parry, 2003). His reasoning was that scientific knowledge, *episteme theoretike*, concerns the underlying rules and principles governing why and how something happens whereas craft, *techne*, deals with everyday practice. Deriving *episteme theoretike* required scholars, through their careful and systematic inquiry, to clarify universal truths and in Tenkasi and Hay's words (2008: 51) 'causal laws that are universally applicable to events and situations'.

However, Aristotle would later re-examine this division in his reflections on the nature of knowledge in the classic work *Metaphysics*. Here, Aristotle shifted his attention from the pursuit of generalizable knowledge as the ultimate end to consider practical action or 'actionable knowledge', *phronesis*, which can both solve practical problems and, in turn, inform generalizable knowledge. Dunne (1993) provides a rich discussion of Aristotle's notion of *phronesis*, showing how the bedrock of true understanding emanates from, and appropriate action is guided through, the creative integration of experience and craft, and theory. Aristotle argued that true knowledge of events and situations, especially as it concerns practical action, involves knowledge of both the experience and craft, *empeiria* and *techne*, derived from those experiences, as well as universal principles, or *episteme theoretike* (that may apply to those settings). Aristotle further contrasts individuals with *empeiria, techne and episteme* with the scholar, the *lógios*, who has only *episteme* and relies on the rational accounting of why things happen without a basis in experience or craft. According to Aristotle, *lógios* are ineffective in producing *phronesis*. Aristotle (1961: 981b) explains:

> ... experience, like action or production, deals with things severally as concrete individuals, whereas art deals with them generally. ... If then someone lacking experience, but knowing the general principles of the art [of medicine], sizes up a situation as a whole, he will often, because he is ignorant of the individuals within that whole, miss the mark and fail to cure; for it is the individuals who must be cured.

Though *phronesis* was highly valued in certain non-Western spheres, it was Aristotle's first legacy of separation that most subsequent Western philosophers and scientists carried forward through recent decades. Other Greek philosophers, such as Plotinus, found little use for *techne* because it did not reveal underlying rules and principles governing why and how something happens beyond a single event or instance. Later philosophers such as John Locke, David Hume, Auguste Comte and, even more recently, Karl Popper, also perpetuated Aristotle's legacy of separation, an orientation which, as Levin and Greenwood (2016) and Shani et al. (2017) describe, eventually became institutionalized in Western universities and the construct of science.

From Aristotle's Legacies to Dewey, Collier and Lewin

The philosophical debate about 'knowledge' and 'knowledge creation process' continues as we write this book (and is likely to continue into the distant future). Capturing the magnitude of the evolution and debate is beyond the scope of this chapter. To bridge a few thousand years of insights, we can argue that the emerging scientific ethos that is built into the separation of thought and action, contradicts Aristotle's ontology of *praxis*. The counter argument that we are what we regularly do seems to be at the core of what John Dewey, the American philosopher who wrote extensively about the need to democratize education, wrote. John Collier, the commissioner of American Indian Affairs, shared the same view as he wrote extensively about the need for a participative approach in order to improve race relations. A similar argument was made by Kurt Lewin, who wrote about the impact of participative research approaches on practice and knowledge creation. As Pasmore (2001) discusses, the work of Dewey, Collier and Lewin is what propelled the recent progression towards a more collaborative research process.

Dewey, in his book, *How We Think* (1933) captures five phases of reflective thinking, namely suggestions, intellectualization, hypothesizing, reasoning and testing hypothesis in action. Understanding thinking, a practical challenge for both scholars and practitioners, seems to trigger for Dewey the need to develop a deeper level understanding of the complex dynamics that are at play, around which the researcher can formulate the hypothesis *together* with the practitioner regarding the cause and effect between the possible variables (elements) that might shape the situational context. For Dewey, practical problems required practical solutions that can be developed through collective inquiry. Dewey did not create the term 'action research'. The credit is held jointly by John Collier and Kurt Lewin, each of whom worked independently addressing different issues, coming at it from different academic disciplines.

As Neilsen (2006) describes, Collier was a commissioner of American Indian Affairs from 1933 to 1945 and worked at trying to improve race relations between whites and Native Americans and, at the same time, study the collaborative change process. After some study and many conversations he came to the realization that problems in ethnic relations could not be overcome by regulations, rules and legal enforcement. Collier and his team coined the term action research as a programme of collaborative research in which representatives of all the parties involved participated in exploring potential causes, carried out systematic data collection and implemented experimentations to reduce the racial tensions. He argued that the only way to impact the current complex dynamics is by having the parties themselves participate in understanding the issues and implemented solutions that they generated. He believed strongly that action research that is conducted as a joint effort between social scientists and laypersons is the most critical tool in changing behaviour in ethnic relations. For him, traditional research can produce insightful observation but is unlikely to change deep-seated beliefs. Creating a context in which the parties involved can engage in a dialogue based on scientifically generated data that they helped create would enhance change in race relations. Kurt Lewin is considered to be the father of social psychology and his influence is everywhere in contemporary management. We expand on his seminal contribution to action research in the following sections.

Both Kurt Lewin and John Collier coined the term action research. The two worked in parallel, around the same period, in two very different spheres. Yet, students of action research recognize Lewin only as the person who created the term. His early ideas about the value of democracy, engagement and participation in the discovery process impacted his scholarly work and all those that surrounded him. Early experiments that examined the impact of different methods to influence behaviour cemented his view that action research as a tool could advance science while at the same time address practical societal problems. Lewin's contribution in incorporating action research to address challenges at the workplace started after the Second World War based on work that was conducted with Harwood Manufacturing Company.

Alex Bavelas, one of Lewin's students at the University of Iowa, worked with Harwood Manufacturing Company on exploring ways to enhance productivity. Lewin (2016) presents Bavelas' account of the action research study. Lewin's orientation and convictions about the potential added value of engaging workers and making them full partners in the study led to the utilization of action research as a methodology in the study. Workers were invited to contribute ideas and take part in the experimentations with different methods to improve productivity. The conditions that they created resulted in the development of a learning context where workers were encouraged to experiment with different methods, collect data about the process and document results. They then discussed the insights with others and proposed methods that they felt would have the most impact. Follow-up studies by Coch and French (1948) continued the experimentation at Harwood, using collaboration and engagement as ways to reduce resistance for change. They demonstrated that more participative management methods, such as action research, were more effective than traditional approaches to change while in parallel generating new theoretical insights. Burnes (2007) views the Harwood studies as the foundation stone of organization development as action research.

Lewin's insights set the stage for a new approach to both the management of change and inquiry. It triggered the development of whole fields of research and practice, such as organization development, community development, global social change, adult learning, and management development. Kurt Lewin and Eric Trist founded the journal *Human Relations* in 1948 as a way to disseminate scholarly work that is more collaborative in nature. Other journals such as the *Journal of Applied Behavioral Science* and those that have action research in their titles, such as *System Practice and Action Research, International Journal of Action Research, Action Research, and Action Learning: Research and Practice* have continued this tradition.

ORGANIZATION DEVELOPMENT

The term organization development (commonly referred to as OD) refers to an approach to organizational change that is a philosophy, a professional field of social action, a mode of scientific inquiry and an array of techniques to enable change to take place in organizations. It is understood to be different from organizational development, the latter referring to the general development of organizations and paralleling terms like personal development and community development. Organization development is understood to refer to a specific values-based approach that has its roots in the work of Kurt Lewin and which is deeply imbedded in action research. Definitions of OD vary but they tend to comprise the following elements in one form or other: that OD is a long-term effort whose aim is to improve an organization's processes of renewing itself through envisioning its future, structuring itself appropriately and being able to solve problems. OD places special emphasis on an ongoing management of organizational culture, particularly in work teams and interdepartmental configurations. It may utilize an external OD consultant who works in a facilitator role, rather than an expert advisor role.

Organization development builds on all the major developments of organization theory and the interface of organizations with the people who work in them. Some of the experiments and research which are more directly related to the emergence of organization development as a distinctive approach to managing planned change are: (1) the work of Kurt Lewin on re-education, planned change, field theory, the stages of change, action research and his seminal work on group dynamics; (2) the work of Eric Trist and his associates in the Tavistock Institute in the UK on coal mining in Durham which led to an understanding of how technology and people are interdependent and how organizations are sociotechnical systems; (3) the client-centred approach to helping individuals make their own personal change pioneered by Carl Rogers, and developed by Edgar Schein; and (4) the approaches to surveying organizations developed by Rensis Likert and his colleagues in Michigan.

Theoretical Foundations of Action Research in Organization Development

Action research is embedded in the tradition of organization development as a collaborative, interventionist form of research that developed from the work of Collier and Lewin. For both Collier and Lewin, it was not enough to try to explain things; one also had to try to change them. Changing any system required basic understanding of the entity and its dynamic interface with its environment. Schein (2010) reflected on Lewin's contribution and noted that Lewin's insights led to the development of action research and the powerful notion that human systems could only be understood and changed if one involved the members of the system in the inquiry process itself. So the tradition of involving the members of an organization in the change process which is the hallmark of organization development (OD), Schein continued, originated in a scientific premise that this is the way a) to get better data and b) to effect change. Action research was based on two assumptions which are the cornerstones of OD. One is that involving the clients or learners in their own learning not only produces better learning but also more valid data about how the system really works. The other is that one only understands a system when one tries to change it, as changing human systems often involves variables which cannot be controlled by traditional research methods.

The early approaches in OD placed a great deal of emphasis on individual and group development and then extended into working with large, complex systems and engaging with issues of strategy, leadership, organizational design, technology, human resource development, organizational learning and latterly sustainability. As Coghlan (2015) describes, in the 1960s, '70s and '80s organization development followed an action research model that entailed a cyclical process of consciously and deliberately a) diagnosing the situation, b) planning action, c) taking action, d) evaluating the action, leading to further diagnosing, planning and so on. The second dimension is that OD was collaborative, in that, with the help of a consultant/facilitator, the members of the system participated actively in the cyclical process. It engaged people as participants in seeking ideas, planning, taking actions, reviewing outcomes and learning what worked and did not work, and why. This approach was in stark contrast to programmed approaches that mandated following pre-designed steps and which tended not to be open to alteration. These latter approaches were based on the assumption that the system should adopt the entire package as designed. OD was based on assumptions that each system is unique and that a change process has to be designed with that uniqueness in mind and adapted in the light of ongoing experience and emergent learning.

Organization development became established as a process for building healthy, high-performance organizations and for improving and realizing the full potential and self-renewing capabilities of organizations, groups and individuals. It was also an education-based strategy that uses a positive and constructive approach to successfully leading and managing change. Now it is understood to be an interdisciplinary approach that draws primarily from the applied behavioural sciences and uses understanding of business and the influence of technology on organizations. It is values-driven and seeks to instil values and build cultures that bring out the best in organizations and people and to encourage open, straightforward, helpful, ethical and increasingly self-directing behaviour. It is a facilitative process that helps others discover and find solutions to their own issues. It relies on a systems perspective of organizations that considers all aspects of an organization and its interrelated parts. It is a data-driven, action-oriented approach that includes assessing reality and involving key stakeholders in evaluating results, exploring what is possible and planning further action. It is a collaborative top-down, bottom-up process that recognizes the importance of building the commitment and leadership of top-level decision makers and involving all stakeholders in the change process. It focuses on both process (how things are done) and content (what is done), recognizing the importance of both. It is often guided and facilitated by professionally trained change agents, both external and internal. It is committed to the transfer of knowledge and skills and to creating learning organizations where organizations and their members are continuously learning, sharing knowledge and improving the organization. Finally, it emphasizes the importance of planned, lasting and sustained change, rather than the quick fix, while at the same time developing the organization's ability to adapt to changing times.

New forms of OD have emerged in the late twentieth century, influenced by quantum physics and living systems theory. These approaches understand systems as webs of relationships rather than as mechanical systems and view organizations as meaning-making systems. Accordingly, contemporary OD views reality as socially constructed with multiple realities which are socially negotiated, rather than as a single objective reality that may be diagnosed. Data collection is less about applying objective problem-solving methods and more about raising collective awareness and generating new possibilities which lead to change. Contemporary OD emphasizes changing the conversation in organizations by surfacing, legitimating and learning from multiple perspectives and generating new images and narratives on which people can act. Accordingly, the focus of OD is to create the space for changing the conversation. Creating spaces for dialogue and the exploration of different design options, by its very nature, brings to the forefront the design perspective, which we will discuss briefly in a later section.

Where might organization development through action research fit in the overall scheme of research approaches? Our perspective is that organization development through action research fits with the notion of Mode 2 knowledge production as proposed by Gibbons and his colleagues (1994, Nowotny et al. (2001)). In brief, the distinction between Mode 1 and Mode 2 knowledge production is that Mode 1 research accords with what we generally mean by the term 'science'. This is typically research that arises from the academic agenda and is conducted within a singular discipline and is accountable to that discipline. The aim of the research is to produce universal knowledge and build and test theory within a disciplinary field. The data are context free and validated by logic, measurement and consistency of prediction and control. The role of the researcher is that of an observer and the relationship to the setting is detached and neutral. In contrast, in Mode 2 knowledge production there is no such division between knowledge production and application. It is transdisciplinary, mobilizing a range of theoretical perspectives and practical methodologies to solve problems. It is dialogical and reflexive as participants engage together and are attentive to continuous learning. In summary, Mode 2 knowledge production combines theoretical knowledge with applied, practical knowledge to solve particular scientific and organizational problems. It is engaged with achieving concrete results by creating actionable knowledge that can advance organizational causes. Action research fits the characteristics for Mode 2 knowledge production.

A specific formulation of organization development through action research is found in the notion of 'dialogic' OD. Bushe and Marshak (2015) describe how understanding that organizations comprise multiple perspectives and meanings, rather than a single technical reality, leads to an emphasis on changing the conversation by surfacing, legitimating and learning from multiple perspectives and generating new images and narratives on which people can act. Data collection is less about applying objective problem-solving methods and more about raising collective awareness and generating new possibilities which lead to change. Accordingly, the focus of OD through action research is to create the space for changing the conversation. In this way, dialogic OD is a form of Mode 2 knowledge production. As we introduced above, it accords with the notion of the action researcher as one who helps the conversations take place that lead to change.

Contrary to the above and from a more critical perspective, in the 85 years since Lewin began to think about action research as a tool for change and learning, action research as a new paradigm is yet to be fully accepted. Some argue that while action research continues to exist and to be practised around the globe, it is still viewed as an alternative paradigm and continuously competing with legitimacy in the face of the same traditional forces that faced Lewin. A promising positive force in the practice of action research and the further development of the action research paradigm is the emerging of post-graduate programmes that encourage the conduct of action research-based dissertation and thesis projects. The utilization of an insider action researcher (part-time graduate student) or outsider action researcher (full-time graduate student with external expert support), or a team of insider and outsider action researchers in the conduct of an action research, seems to be generating a new wave of legitimacy in the worlds of practice and academia.

Questions for Reflection

Returning to Kevin's situation and his sense of the opportunity to combine his forthcoming managerial challenge with his MBA dissertation, can you understand the change process in which he was engaged? What appear to be some of the challenges that Kevin's company is experiencing? Thinking about your potential idea for the project in a company/system that you might want to consider for your dissertation, what is your sense of its context? What appear to be some of the challenges that the company is experiencing? Have you any initial ideas about possible action plans? What might be some possible actions? What kind of data might you want to collect? How might the data collection take place and by whom? What might be possible arenas for dialogue? Who might be the potential partners for the dialogue? How would you go about evaluating the action? What data might you capture so that you could conduct an evaluation of the action? Write a reflection on your provisional answers to these questions in your reflective journal.

SOCIOTECHNICAL SYSTEMS

Organizations are viewed as complex adaptive systems. As Miller and Page (2007) discuss, no two systems are alike. As Pasmore (1988) explores, each system is unique, not easy to decipher, navigate or understand. Mohrman and Shani (2011) argue that systems exist within a context and, in order for the system to survive and be successful over time, adaptation to the ever-changing context is required. A conceptual framework of an organization can be of great help. In this volume we advance the sociotechnical system that can serve as a basic conceptual framework that may guide understanding and help decipher the context within which an action research project can evolve.

As was mentioned earlier, sociotechnical systems theory of organizations, organization design, management and organizational change has had a major impact on the evolution of action research. The initial work was conducted at the Tavistock Institute in the UK and the workplace democracy projects in Scandinavia attempted to address major challenges in the workplace while simultaneously generating new theoretical insights. Sociotechnical systems thinking provides a broad framework to understand systems.

Eric Trist (1982), one of the pioneers of sociotechnical thinking, understood that, at the most basic level, a sociotechnical system (STS) is embedded in the view that organizations are made up of people who produce products or services using some technology. As such, as Pasmore (1988 and 1994) describes, the STS approach attempts to combine the social subsystem (people), the technical subsystem (machines and technology) and the environmental supersystem into a synergistic system. Authors such as Emery (1959), Cummings (1980) and Hanna (1988) emphasize how joint optimization, the ultimate desire in STS, states that an organization will function optimally only if the social and technological subsystems of the organization are designed to fit the demands of each other and the environment. Shani and Elliott (1989) discuss how the STS approach emphasizes the need for compatible integration between the organization's social and technical subsystems to ensure organizational effectiveness. Since its inception in the 1950s, as Adler and Docherty (1998) and Van Eijnatten et al. (2008) identify, three major sociotechnical system subfields emerged: STS theory, STS design, and STS change and development.

Successful STS design focuses on an 'open' interface with the environment the organization faces. This implies that the ability of the organization to effectively match its social and technical subsystems relies on the degree of openness or contact the organization maintains with the environment. Organizational competitiveness necessitates the need for organizations to maintain environmental sensing and scanning mechanisms such that the organization will be able to plan and adapt according to anticipated and unanticipated changes. Changes in any one of the subsystems will disturb the status quo and should result in the realignment of the entire organization. As Van Eijnatten et al. (2008) demonstrate, utilizing design thinking is at the route of the sociotechnical system design, a point we explore later in this chapter.

In the context of organization development, the STS planned change intervention is based on the action research or collaborative research philosophy. As such, the STS change endeavour is participatory, co-inquiry-based, client- and organization-owned, and scientifically executed and is viewed as one of the accepted perspectives in the field of organization development and change.

Questions for Reflection

Returning to Kevin's situation and his sense of the opportunity to combine his forthcoming managerial challenge with his MBA dissertation, can you reflect and identify the key features of his systems? What are some of the key environmental factors that he needs to consider? What are some of the key elements of the social subsystem? Of the technological subsystem? Are there any other contextual factors that seem to be potentially relevant to the project? As you think about your potential idea for a topic that you might want to consider for your dissertation, what are some of the key features of sociotechnical systems in which you might carry out an action research project? What are some of the key environmental factors that you need to consider? What are some of the key elements of the social subsystem? Of the technological subsystem? Are there any other contextual factors that seem to be potentially relevant to the project? Write a reflection on your provisional answers to these questions in your reflective journal.

DESIGN THINKING

As Shani and Docherty (2003) describe, the impact of system complexity coupled with the emerging need to become more innovative and adaptable brought the exploration of design thinking to the forefront. The concept of design thinking evolved over the past decade in a few disciplines, such as architecture, engineering design, and business. At the most basic level, as Martin (2009) describes, design thinking means thinking as a designer would. According to Tim Brown (2008: 85), 'design thinking is a discipline that uses the designer's sensitivity and methods to match people's needs with what is technologically feasible and what a viable business strategy can convert into customer value and market opportunity'. Schön (1983) argues that the common denominator of the increasingly growing design professions family is that all designers are engaged in converting actual to preferred situations via design thinking.

Action research projects could be designed and managed in various ways. The design of an action research project is viewed as a rational choice among alternatives that deploy variation of inductive, deductive and abductive logics. As Lillrank et al. (2001) discuss, alternative choices can be made about the nature of the structural configurations, processes and activities. They can also be made in terms of the orientation for the collaborative development of the topic to be studied, namely inside-out. Hanna (1988) provides an account of his exploration of insider-outsider perspectives in his insider work.

The design perspective suggests further that the action researcher actively looks for data points, challenges accepted assumptions, and infers possible new ways to understand a situation or a challenge. From a design perspective, the action researcher needs to make sure that the project meets basic requirements: namely, the issue/s to be addressed and its definition and scope match what is feasible in the system based on current practices and business challenges; and the action research process and inquiry orientation must make sense within the specific business context and dynamics.

Questions for Reflection

Thinking about your potential idea for the project in the company/system that you might want to consider for your dissertation, how might you begin to frame the topic? What are some of the potential challenges that you see as an outsider? What might be some of the challenges that insiders are experiencing? What might be topics of interest that might fit both you as an outsider and the insiders' view? What might be some of the alternative action research mechanisms (structures, processes and activities) that you would want to explore? How would you go about investigating the potential fit between the action research mechanisms and the organization capability to optimize them? What might be possible arenas for dialogue? How would you go about designing and establishing them? Write a reflection on your provisional answers to these questions in your reflective journal.

CYCLES OF ACTION AND REFLECTION

As action research takes place in real time and in the present tense and is focused on generating practical knowing, its core process is captured by the notion of cycles of action and reflection. In its original and simplest form, Lewin (1997) presented the action research cycle as comprising a pre-step and three core activities: planning action, taking action and fact-finding:

- The pre-step involves naming the general objective.
- Planning comprises having an overall plan and a decision regarding what the first step to take is.
- Action involves taking that first step.
- Fact-finding involves evaluating the first step, seeing what was learned and creating the basis for correcting the next step.

So, in Lewin's words (1946/1997: 146), there is a continuing 'spiral of steps, each of which is composed of a circle of planning, action and fact-finding about the result of the action.' While these cycles may be presented differently, all presentations capture the essential elements of the original Lewinian framework. In working within the realm of practical knowing where knowing is always incomplete, engaging in and pay-ing attention to these cycles is paramount.

Action research works through a rigorous assessment of the context and purpose of the research and takes place in the present tense, in real time by enacting a cycli-cal four-step process of consciously and deliberately: i) planning, ii) taking action and iii) evaluating the action, leading to iv) further planning as implementing concurrent cycles of action and research. In Figure 1.2, we present an action research cycle com-prising a pre-step and four main steps - constructing, planning action, taking action and evaluating action.

Though such cycles of action and reflection are central to the practice of action research, they need not be enacted in a rigid manner but may find expression in an imaginative and expressive approach. Coghlan and Brannick (2014) present the outcomes of the cycles of action and reflection as generating content, process and premise learning, premise learning being the fruit of critical thinking. We discuss each of the steps in turn.

Pre-step: Context and Purpose

The action research cycle unfolds in real time and requires a clear rationale for action. It begins with seeking an understanding of the context of the project. Why is

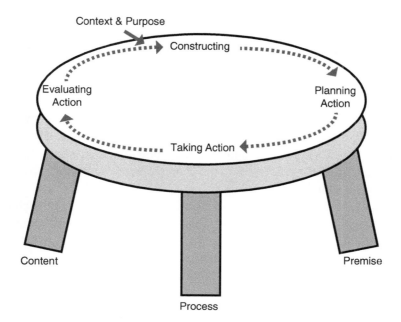

Figure 1.2   Meta-cycle of action research

Source: Coghlan and Brannick, 2014: 13. With permission.

this project necessary or desirable? For whom might it be necessary or desirable? How might it fit the unit's or organization's goals or vision? The action researcher needs to become familiar with the industry in which the firm is competing and the position of the firm within that industry and be able to outline, however provisionally, the intended added value for the organization. An outcome of the pre-step is securing access and consolidating a recognized role for the action researcher. Just because it is necessary for the organization to engage in the proposed action does not mean that it holds the potential to contribute new knowledge of value in research terms. The complementary question is to ask what the rationale for the research is and, in particular, the rationale for the thesis action research project. Another critical consideration in this pre-step is the establishment of collaborative relationships with those who have ownership or need to have ownership of the above questions. A central second-person task in this regard is to develop the group or groups with which you will be working on the project. We will pick up these issues in Chapter 4.

Main Steps

- *Constructing:* Constructing involves naming what the issues are, however provisionally, as a working theme on the basis of which action will be planned and taken. It is a dialogic activity in which the stakeholders of the project engage.
- *Planning action:* Planning action follows from the exploration of the context and purpose of the project, the constructing of the issue and is consistent with what you have identified as critical. It may be that this action planning focuses on a first step or a series of first steps. In Chapter 4 we will describe how you implement the action research project. Again, we emphasize the importance of collaboration in planning action.
- *Taking action:* The firm implements the planned action. This action involves making the desired changes and following through on the plans in collaboration with relevant key members of the organization. Documenting the 'what', the 'how' and the initial impact and/or reactions to the changes as the action takes place is likely to help the collaborative reflection process.
- *Evaluating action:* Evaluation means appraising some aspect of a change situation. Such evaluation is the key to learning. Without evaluation, actions can go on and on regardless of success or failure; errors can proliferate and ineffectiveness and frustration increase. The outcomes of the action, both intended and unintended, are examined with a view to seeing if the original constructing was fitted; if the actions taken matched the constructing; if the action was taken in an appropriate manner; and what feeds into the next cycle of constructing, planning and action. So the cycle continues, as Figure 1.3 demonstrates.

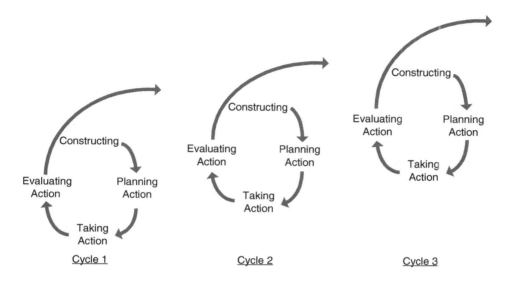

Figure 1.3 Cycles of action and reflection

Source: Coghlan and Brannick, 2014: 11. With permission.

In any action research project there are multiple action research cycles operating concurrently. These cycles typically have different time spans. The entire project may be viewed as one cycle. Within that major cycle, distinct phases may constitute minor cycles and within them specific incidents as further cycles of action and reflection.

While cycles of action and reflection are common in approaches such as in quality management, experiential training and learning, action learning and project management, they are focused on achieving the task. As Whitehead (2005) points out, action research and project management are two sides of the same coin. What makes the cycles in action research different from their use in these approaches is that they are directed to knowledge and theory generation.

The cycles of action and reflection may be seen in Kevin's story.

Box 1.3 Cycles of action and reflection

Kevin could see that his work at building an integrated team would evolve through several cycles of action and reflection. He wanted and hoped that team meetings would not only discuss what was done and how it was done up to now but would also attempt to uncover underlying assumptions, particularly those unquestioned assumptions that lay in the minds of the team members that would likely surface

(Continued)

(Continued)

in the new team setting as troublesome. He would hold a series of meetings with his team that would have the specific purpose of enabling people to share their anxieties and identify and address issues that were identified. For each meeting he would have an agenda and a hoped-for outcome. At a meeting he would propose a topic for discussion and the team members, in discussing that topic, would share their perspective on the future situation, their anxieties about it and what might be done. From that meeting tasks would emerge, and Kevin would work with individuals on those tasks before the next meeting. There were cycles of meeting, discussions and work between the meetings from which other issues would emerge and be addressed at the next meeting. An example of such a cycle was how Kevin and the team explored the way in which the team currently operated an informal task assignment system. If a problem arose, an individual would take it upon himself to address it without being formally assigned and the problem would be addressed without being documented. In the new enlarged setting, there would need to be formalised role assignment and documentation. While this looked good on paper, the team members were anxious about the possible loss of their collaborative spirit through its replacement with a bureaucratic system.

Questions for Reflection

As you consider your proposed action research study, how might you design it to work in cycles of action and reflection? What might be some of the challenges that you could face in each of the phases in the cycles? How might you overcome some of the possible emerging challenges? How might you build ongoing collaborative reflection into the process, given that it is likely that you will engage vigorously in the action but resist having to take time to reflect? Write a reflection on your provisional answers to these questions in your reflective journal.

REFLECTION

Throughout this book we invite you to pause and apply the theory you are reading to your action research dissertation. We are calling these pauses *'Questions for Reflection'*. Reflection is normally explained as a process of standing back from experience to question it and to have insights. It involves not simply describing experience but also doing some analysis through exploring links between behaviour and outcomes, questioning ideas and assumptions seeking understanding. Reflection can be done after the fact where you can reflect on an incident after it has taken place. This is usually referred to as reflection-after- or reflection-on-action. The problem with reflection-on-action is that the incident is over and perhaps nothing can be done now. The hoped-for skill is to learn to reflect-in-action, where, by being attentive to events as they are taking place, you can say or do something that shapes the direction of what is taking place.

The knowledge generated through action research emerges from reflection in and on the cycles of action and reflection. Coghlan and Brannick (2014) use the term 'meta-learning' in describing three forms of reflection: content, process and premise in an action research context. *Content* reflection is where you and others think about the issues, what is happening and so on. *Process* reflection is where you and others think about strategies, phases, procedures and how things are being done. *Premise* reflection is where you and others critique your underlying assumptions and per-spectives. In action research, all three forms of reflection are critical. When content, process and premise reflections are applied to your action research project, they form meta-learning, that is, learning about learning. It is the dynamic of this reflection on reflection that enables action research to be more than everyday problem solving or project management.

Keeping a Reflective Journal

It is standard practice and highly recommended that you keep a reflective journal during the progress of your action research work. A reflective journal is a record of events, thoughts and feelings about the events of the action research as they occur. It is like a diary but it is oriented towards reflection and learning, hence oriented towards deliberative thought and analysis related to practice, and so it is a vehicle for reflection. Essentially a reflective journal captures:

1. What took place on a particular occasion (what you and others said and did)
2. What you thought and felt about what happened
3. What your reflection is on both of the above.

While reflective journals may be highly structured or unstructured, it is useful to have some structure so as to keep track of your questions and learning over the period of your action research work. A useful format might be:

1. Recount an incident – what, who said and did what, what you thought and felt ...
2. What question arises for you from that incident?
3. What insights have you into that incident? About the situation? About you?
4. Can you test or have you tested those insights? Question your own thinking?
5. Then/now what?

It is important that journal entries are linked to one another so that your reflection on a particular incident finds echoes in your reflection on other incidents, where you might show how you learned from an earlier incident or that you have not and that that sets up a further question and inquiry. A reflective journal maps reflection over time as well as at a particular time. Your reflective journal is the appropriate location for the reflections that you write in answer to the *Questions for Reflection* that feature in this and other chapters. Moon (1999) and Basset (2013) provide more detailed introductions to keeping a reflective journal.

CORE AND DISSERTATION PROJECTS

When you are enrolled in an academic education programme, such as one leading to a masters degree, it is useful to note that typically there are two action research projects co-existing in parallel, a learning project and a research project, as McKay and Marshall (2001) put it. Zuber-Skerritt and Perry (2002) describe these as the *core* project and the *thesis* project. First, there is the *core* action research project which is the project on which you are working within the organization. This project has its own identity as addressing a real issue within the organization and is driven by organizational needs and may proceed, irrespective of whether or not it is being studied. It represents an opportunity for you to tap into an already active agenda for action and change. The project may also be funded externally and carry with it a timescale and deliverables which are independent of the academic research programme.

Second, there is the *dissertation* or *thesis* action research project. This project involves your inquiry into the core project. Here, at the outset, you are assessing whether or not there is a viable dissertation in this organizational project that is the core project. You evaluate the subject of the change in light of both its practical challenge and its potential to deliver a dissertation. This evaluation involves a sense of the relevant literature and your hoped-for contribution. The distinction between the *core* project and the *dissertation* project is useful as it is the *dissertation* project which will be submitted for examination, rather than the core project. In summary, at the outset you assess the rationale for action (that the *core* project is worth doing) and the rationale for research (that it is worth researching).

In summary, the *core* project is the organizational project. The *dissertation* project is your account of the core project enhanced by your literature and methodology that together offer a contribution to actionable knowledge and get you your masters degree.

The two projects are evident in Kevin's work.

Box 1.4   Core and dissertation projects

With regard to the *core* and *dissertation* projects of his work, Kevin was acutely aware of his dual challenge. Not only did he have to help his existing team prepare for the arrival of the new members from the other organization (the *core* project), he also had to write a dissertation on the preparation process that would provide an understanding of what worked or did not – and how – and be awarded a desired MBA for this written work (the *dissertation* project).

Questions for Reflection

Standing back from Kevin's identification of the two projects in his case, can you distinguish between your *core* and *dissertation* projects? How does this distinction help you design your action research work? Whom in the organization, that you trust and who knows the organization and its dynamics well, can you talk with (consult) about the possible distinction between the two and how can each be managed? Might there be specific mechanisms that you may put in place to ensure the progress of both? Write a reflection on your provisional answers to these questions in your reflective journal.

THE REMAINDER OF THIS BOOK

Having provided you with an introduction to action research through a definition, theoretical foundations and history, we now develop these core ideas. In Chapter 2 we elaborate the foundations of action research by grounding action research in the realm of practical knowing, that is the knowing which is focused on practical concerns and which lead to improved actions. We locate the enactment of action research in three practices: first, second and third person. Each of these play a central role in your dissertation as you work with others to address the practical issues confronting your organization/department, learn about yourself as you enact the role of action researcher and generate and articulate knowledge that is solidly based in these two practices which is of use to others. We show how action research has many expressions or modalities, which provide insights into different ways of enacting action research. In Chapter 3 we develop the idea introduced in this chapter of action research integrating action and research in the service of addressing a real organizational issue and generating actionable knowledge. We discuss what action research involves and we apply the definition provided earlier in this chapter to the *core* and *dissertation* action research project in terms of design and gaining access. Chapter 4 describes how your action research engages you in seven core activities: grounding the purpose and a rationale of the research; describing the business, social and academic context of the research; articulating the methodology, methods and mechanisms of action; framing the issue to be addressed and the design to be followed; carrying out the action research process, capturing the narrative of what took place and its outcomes; reflecting on the narrative and outcomes; and exploring how the particular situated action research project may be discussed and extrapolated to a theory-based context beyond your local situation.

Chapter 5 provides a selection of published action research studies to demonstrate the breadth of work across the range of sectors, business functions/disciplines and modalities. As well as demonstrating the wide range across industries and business functions/disciplines, the selection shows the practical nature of the issues addressed and the contribution to knowledge generated through the various actions. Chapter 6 draws together the themes of the preceding five chapters and encapsulates the strengths and limitations of action research, under what conditions it works or does not work, what its contribution is, and we point to how your dissertation might be successful.

SUMMARY

This chapter has presented an introduction to action research as an approach to research that does not distinguish between research and action; it addresses the theme of *research in action*. It works at gathering and generating data with practitioners who want to improve their organizations and it works through cycles of constructing the issues, planning action to address them, taking action, evaluating the actions and then constructing the next cycles. Enactment of the cycles challenges the emergence of content, process and premise issues for the thesis project. Chapter 4 will elaborate on these processes.

In this chapter we have located action research in the history of the tension between knowledge and practice. Action research does not recognize this distinction and explicitly integrates them. We have outlined briefly the core tenets of action research in Aristotle, Dewey, Collier and Lewin. We introduced three conceptual pillars of action research, namely an approach to organizational change, called organization development (OD), sociotechnical systems and design thinking. Organization development was defined as a collaborative, interventionist form of research, grounded in action research. Organization development through action research has the capacity to bridge the knowledge-practice gap that besets contemporary organization studies.

The sociotechnical system was presented as a broad conceptual map to sort out the complex nature of organizations as adaptive systems within which an action research project is likely to reside. The design perspective highlighted the unique design role of the action researcher. From this perspective the action researcher is viewed as a designer that makes choices among alternatives and as such carries the responsibility of making sure that the issue to be addressed, its definition and scope match what is feasible in the system based on current practices and business challenges. An integral part of the design perspective is to lead the collaborative decision about choices among alternative structural configurations, processes and procedures within which the action research project resides. These are key elements that when put together created a field of knowledge and practice and which represent tensions that go back centuries. For concise explanations of underlying philosophies of action research as well as methodologies, methods and tools, the *SAGE Encyclopedia of Action Research* (2014) is an invaluable resource.

2

UNDERSTANDING ACTION RESEARCH

INTRODUCTION

In the previous chapter we introduced action research and tracked its roots in Aristotelian philosophy through Lewin's social psychology and organization development. As we pointed out, addressing the tensions between basic knowledge production and action is not new. As we referenced in Chapter 1, Gibbons et al. (1994) and Nowotny et al. (2001) framed this tension in terms of Mode 1 and Mode 2 knowledge production, a distinction which MacLean et al. (2002) brought to the field of management and organization studies. This separation of knowledge and practice and of rigour and relevance, which emerged in academia during the first half of the twentieth century, divides management scholars and practitioners. More recently, some management scholars, such as Argyris et al. (1985), Van de Ven (2007) and Lawler and Mohrman (2011), have re-examined this division, recognizing the potential of research orientations that combine basic research with practice to solve problems of organizational, societal and scientific concern. As Shani et al. (2008) and Coghlan and Brannick (2014) explore, action research, which draws on the spirit of early management scholarship, provides a paradigm for bridging the gap that exists between the production of basic knowledge and practice.

Action research is grounded in what Schein (2008) calls a 'clinical perspective'. By a 'clinical perspective' he means questioning and studying events that arouse your curiosity. Are there problems and anomalies that are difficult to explain? Here you can look back on incidents and ask critical questions as to how some events or incidents inhibit the organization from functioning effectively. You might, for example, study what happened when management enacted a change, such as changing the roster or introducing new technology. Schein (2013a) does not see the clinician in the mode of the medical expert who diagnoses and prescribes, but rather as a sort of organizational therapist who works with the system to enable it to change itself. In the remainder of this book we will work from a 'clinical' perspective through encouraging you to be attentive to what is going on in the organization and to be questioning of what puzzles you, particularly through the process of change.

WAYS OF KNOWING

There are different ways in which we know. We are familiar with these; how, for example, when we listen to music, read poetry or visit an art gallery, we are in an aesthetic form of knowing as we appreciate melodies and harmonies, language or visual representations. We engage in a different way of knowing when we are engaged in science and are studying technical readings or assessing financial reports. Here we adopt a scientific form of knowing as we check data, weigh evidence and conclusions. Relational knowing is what we draw on when we work with someone or form a friendship. Then there is the realm of practical knowing that enables us to manage our everyday activities, to which we apply our intelligence to practical tasks.

The different approaches to research reflect different ways of knowing. You may be familiar with the philosophy of research that is based on positivist science. Table 2.1 provides an overview of the three main research approaches: positivist science, interpretist and action research. Positivist science is based on the natural sciences and

Table 2.1 Comparing forms of research

	Positivist science	*Interpretist*	*Action research*
Research question	What can be proven?	What is interesting?	What is useful?
Data gathering methods	Detached	Participation observation	Active engagement
Data analysis	Statistical	Contextual	Participatory
Qualification	Internal	External and internal validity	Experiential
Quality	Validity	Credibility	Actionability
Role of researcher	Detached	Detached	Engaged
Audience	Academics	Academics	Academics and practitioners

formulates an objective science by separating fact from value and by asserting that genuine knowledge is what is obtained through the scientific method of hypothesis formulation, investigation and verification through careful control and measurement. The intended audience is academic and the researcher plays a detached role. In contrast, interpretist approaches, found in case studies, explore the meanings that organizational members hold about events in the organization. The work is qualified or validated through external and internal validity. The intended audience is academic and the researcher plays a participant observer role. In both the positivist and interpretist traditions of research, the emphasis is on knowledge creation, to an explicit exclusion of action. As we introduced in Chapter 1, action research constitutes a different form of research that is based on radically different foundations, namely of action and participation. Accordingly, the common classification of research approaches into quantitative and qualitative, and specifically classifying action research as a form of qualitative, is not only meaningless but is also incorrect. Susman and Evered (1978: 601) argue that action research 'constitutes a kind of science with a different epistemology that produces a different kind of knowledge, a knowledge that is contingent on the particular situation and which develops the capacity of members of organizations to solve their own problems'. In using the term 'scientific', there is a need to move away from adopting frameworks from natural sciences in order to engage with the world of practice. When Torbert (1991: 220) refers to 'a kind of scientific inquiry conducted in everyday life' and Argyris et al. (1985: 4) to 'a science of practice', they are extending the normal connotations associated with the term 'science'.

As Coghlan (2011) describes, action research contributes to the realm of practical knowing. It focuses on organizational improvement and change and seeks to contribute knowledge that is actionable, and not merely theoretical. Coghlan (2016) elaborates on how the characteristics of the realm of practical knowing are that a) our knowing in this mode is concerned with the everyday concerns of human living, b) much of our knowing in this mode is socially derived, constructed and reconstructed continuously, c) we need to attend to the uniqueness of each situation and d) our practical knowing and action are driven by values and are fundamentally ethical in that as we take practical action we are constantly making judgements about what is the appropriate or best thing to do. We now elaborate on these four characteristics of practical knowing:

The everyday concerns of human living

Action research does not pursue knowledge for its own sake, but it pursues actions that are judged to be worthwhile. In the context of business and management, the everyday practical concerns are about issues such as survival, productivity, effectiveness, customer service, improvement and change. Those who undertake action research do so not merely to study such issues but to improve or transform them.

Socially constructed

Action research has long been comfortable with understanding that our thinking and the creation of our institutions and their operations are socially constructed, that is, they are creations of the human mind and are designed and run to achieve intended purposes. Consequently, when action researchers work with other people they see that others interpret situations differently and accordingly engage in dialogical and collaborative activities which seek to build common understanding and consensual collaborative action.

Attending to the uniqueness of each situation

The third characteristic of practical knowing is that it requires attentiveness to the uniqueness of each situation. This particular characteristic of practical knowing means that knowing varies from place to place and from situation to situation. What is familiar in one place may be unfamiliar in another. What works in one setting may not work in another. No two situations are identical. A remembered set of insights is only approximately appropriate to the new situation. They are insights into situations which are similar but not identical. Therefore, our practical knowing needs to be differentiated for each specific situation and, as Coghlan and Shani (2017) explore, action researchers need to be attentive in the present tense and engage in the cycles of action and reflection outlined in the previous chapter.

Values driven and ethical

Practical action is driven by values that are what we judge to be worth doing, and so is fundamentally ethical in how values are identified, choices are made and actions are taken. Reason (2006) points out that action research is characteristically full of choices. As it is conducted in the present tense, attentiveness to these choices and their consequences, and being transparent about them are significant for considering the quality of action research. Reason argues that action researchers need to be aware of the choices they face and make them clear and transparent to themselves and to those with whom they are engaging in inquiry and to those to whom they present their research in writing or presentations.

Heron and Reason (1997) argue that practical knowing is primary as it integrates other forms of knowing. We draw on the knowledge created by others and use it intelligently, for example, when we cook a meal. The recipe in the cookbook provides the theory but then we have to apply it intelligently in order that the meal be edible. In our organizational world, we can draw on operations management theory to effect changes in how the operation of the supply chain might be improved, but what to do and how to do it takes us into the realm of practical knowing.

We return to Kevin's story.

Box 2.1 Practical knowing

Kevin's dissertation project lay in the realm of practical knowing. The primary concern was practical, that is to prepare his team for the arrival of the new colleagues. He would have to work with how his team members interpreted the new situation, such as how they were seeing it as a threat and were anxious about it. He would be working in the present tense, that is, being attentive to what his colleagues were saying at meetings, trying to catch the mood in the team and responding appropriately. He had come to terms with the reality of the acquisition, saw its value for the firm and knew that what he had to do was worthwhile and of value to both the firm and to its employees in his section. At the same time, he wanted to help his team members to be at ease with the new situation and to help them enhance their skills and contribution to the firm. He would also generate useful knowledge on how to prepare a merged team for others outside of his section and firm.

Questions for Reflection

Being informed by Kevin's practical orientation and getting back to the initial idea/s that you have had about a possible challenge of interest (captured earlier), what might be the practical knowledge that your action research dissertation might aim to generate? How might it be useful beyond the immediacy of your own firm or department or firm? Write a reflection in your reflective journal on your answers to these questions.

THREE PRACTICES IN ACTION RESEARCH

An integrative approach to research incorporates three practices: first, second and third person. What is meant by these terms is that action research is an engaging process that involves challenges of self-learning (first person), working with others to achieve the task (second person) and making a contribution to knowledge (third person). Traditional research has focused on third-person researchers doing research on third persons and writing a report for other third persons. In a more complete vision of research as presented by action research, authentic third-person research integrates first- and second-person practices.

First-person Practice

As action researchers are themselves agents in the generation of data, it is important that you afford explicit attention to your own learning-in-action. When you, as an action researcher, engage in the action research cycles with others and try to understand and shape what is going on, you are also engaging in your own experiential learning activities, what we call first-person practice. Here, some of the core skills you need as an action researcher are in the areas of self-awareness and sensitivity to what you observe, supported by the conceptual analytic frameworks on which you base your observations and interpretations. Your inquiry can be focused outward (e.g. what is going on in the organization, in the team?) or inward (e.g. what is going on in you?). When you inquire into what is going on, when you show people your train of thought and put forward hypotheses to be tested, when you make suggestions for action, you are generating data. People's responses (as organizational team members, fellow researchers or supervisors) to these interventions generate further data. Your reflective journal aims to capture this learning-in-action as it happens.

A General Empirical Method

The first-person process, whereby you pay attention to how your mind is working as you engage in action research, is the recognizable process of human knowing. As Cronin (2017) demonstrates, if you take the time to ask yourself how you know something, you will notice that knowing involves three steps. First, you attend to an experience and ask a 'what is it?' question. What is that noise? Second, you receive an insight which is an understanding as an answer to your question. That noise sounds like the telephone ringing. Are you correct in this answer? You may or may not be, so you check. Is it so? Having gathered the data you then can, third, seek further evidence and make the judgement that the noise you heard was indeed the telephone ringing. Now you know. You can check this process for yourself. Notice the same steps you go through in doing a Sudoku, a crossword puzzle, solving a practical problem, writing an essay and so on. In each and all of these situations, you go through the same three steps: having an experience, asking a 'what is it?' question, receiving an insight (understanding) and following it up by weighing up the evidence to determine whether your insight is correct or not (judgement), asking an 'is it so?' question. It may not stop here. You may also choose to do something, so you decide to answer the phone. Table 2.2 captures the process.

Human knowing is not any of these operations on their own. All knowing involves experience, understanding and judgement. Of course, you may not always be attentive to experience. You may not ask questions. Understanding may not flow spontaneously from experience. Your insights may be wrong. You may take short cuts and go with the first answer you come up with or the one that is most convenient. Interpretations of data may be superficial, inaccurate, biased; judgements may be flawed. You can

Table 2.2   The operations of human knowing and doing

Experience	Seeing, hearing, smelling, tasting, touching, remembering, imagining, feeling ...
Understanding	Inquiring, understanding, formulating what is being understood
Judgement	Marshalling evidence, testing, judging if it fits the evidence or what is true
Decision/action	Deliberating, valuing, deciding, choosing, taking action, behaving ...

gain insight into these negative manifestations of knowing by the same three-fold process of knowing. The pattern of the three operations is invariant in that it applies to all settings of cognitional activity, whether solving a crossword clue, addressing a problem at work or at home, or engaging in scientific research.

As Cronin (2017) describes, learning to appropriate your intellectual activities means to become aware of them, to be able to identify and distinguish them, to grasp how they are related and to be able to make the process explicit. Accordingly, you not only experience, understand and judge the world around you; you also experience, understand and judge your own process of knowing and learning. The cognitional operations of experience, understanding and judgement form a general empirical method (Table 2.3), which requires you to:

- Be *attentive* to what is going on around you and inside you.
- Be *intelligent* in envisaging possible explanations of those data.
- Be *reasonable* in preferring as probable or certain the explanations which provide the best account for the data.
- Be *responsible* for your actions.

Throughout this book we will remind and challenge you continually as to how you are being attentive, intelligent, reasonable and responsible as you engage in your action research project.

Table 2.3   The general empirical method in action research

Be attentive	To data both outside and inside yourself
Be intelligent	In your understanding
Be reasonable	In your judgements
Be responsible	For your actions

Learning-in-action is grounded in the inquiry–reflection process. It is the key to learning as it enables you as an action researcher to develop an ability to uncover and make explicit to yourself what you planned, discovered and achieved in practice. As we discussed above, in action research, reflection is the activity that integrates action and research and is captured in your reflective journal. Reflection on content, process and premise must be brought into the open so that it goes beyond your privately held, taken-for-granted assumptions and helps you to see how your knowledge is socially constructed. This is what we mean by *first-person practice*. Writers such as Argyris and Schön (1974), Torbert and Associates (2004), Kahneman (2011) and Marshall (2016) present rich frameworks within action research that enable you to attend to your own learning-in-action. Argyris and Schön pay specific attention to how you can make inferences about other people's actions and attribute motives without testing them and they provide techniques for uncovering how you are thinking. Torbert and his associates work in the same vein and offer ways of thinking about how to approach taking action and may engage in different forms of conversation. Kahneman shows how you can engage in faulty thinking by applying causal thinking inappropriately and can jump to conclusions. Marshall demonstrates how to 'live life as inquiry', as she puts it, by bringing a questioning approach to life.

Second-person Practice

Second-person practice addresses your engagement in collaborative work in co-inquiry and shared action with others on issues of mutual concern, through face-to-face dialogue, conversation and joint action. Underpinning second-person practice is an appreciation of others, especially if they appear to hold an adversarial position to you, and you may find yourself thinking of them as awkward, resistant or opposing. Such an appreciative position demands you to be empathic towards them by trying to see the situation as they see it and by trying to value that position as offering a contribution to addressing the issue at hand.

Schein (2009, 2013b) presents three useful ways of engaging with others. His first category is what he calls *pure inquiry*. This is where you listen carefully to others' accounts of their experience of the issues at hand and elicit and explore their stories of what is taking place. Examples of pure inquiry interventions are: Tell me what happened? Who said what to whom? Then what happened? What did you do? Questions such as these enable your co-inquirers to relate their experience and provide the core data of experience. The second type of inquiry is what Schein calls *diagnostic inquiry*, in which you begin to guide your co-inquirers' thinking process by asking questions that elicit their causal thinking. Examples of questions in this mode are: What do you think was going on? How do you understand what took place? The third type of inquiry is what Schein calls *confrontive inquiry*. This is where you share your own ideas and challenge your co-inquirers to think from an alternative perspective. An example in this mode is: Have you thought about X? Might Y be an alternative explanation?

Schein makes the point that if you begin in confrontive mode, you are setting your-self up as the expert by showing that you have (or think you have) the solution. This has the effect of inhibiting the conversation and limiting shared inquiry and shared action. Accordingly, he emphasizes spending more time in pure and diagnostic inquiry modes in order to build co-ownership of the shared task and to draw on the expertise in the group with which you are working.

Third-person Practice

Third-person practice is impersonal and is actualized through the contribution of the action research to an audience beyond those directly involved, such as through dissemination by reporting, publishing and being examined. Your dissertation is a third-person activity in how it is expressed in a document that will be read by an examiner and future students. What action research aims at is an explicit integration of all three practices with action and inquiry.

How does knowledge come from action? The knowledge generated in masters dissertations generally is not expected to be totally new, as would be expected in a doctorate. Bartunek (1983) explores how practice can contribute to already formu-lated theories – by testing and/or elaborating them and by describing or understanding interpretations that arise through interventions. It can point out problem areas that are experienced in practice but that are not adequately addressed in a theory. It can seek to understand underlying patterns through exploring its integrity

It seems that frameworks are useful in making sense of the world. But which frame-works? What do they leave out? How accessible are they to participants? What effect does that have on participation, and in turn on actions? Action research intentionally merges theory with practice on the grounds that actionable knowledge can result from the interplay of knowledge with action. Action research demands an explicit concern with theory that is generated from the conceptualization of the particular experience in ways that are intended to be meaningful to others. We identify three characteristics: situation specific, emergent and incremental:

- Action research does not lend itself to repeatable experimentation – each interven-tion will be different to the last. So, action research projects are *situation specific* and do not aim to create universal knowledge.
- Action research generates *emergent* theory, in which the theory develops from a synthesis of the understanding which emerges from reflection on the core project data and from the use in practice of the body of relevant theories which informed the research purpose. In contrast to positivist science, where the theory to be tested is defined from the outset, theoretical understanding in action research unfolds through the reflections on the action and their outcomes.

- Theory generation in the *core* action research project is *incremental*, moving from the particular to the general in small steps. A *core* action research project unfolds through cycles as the problematic issue(s) being tackled is confronted (or the opportunity exploited) and members of the organization attempt resolution with the help of the action researcher. The enactment of the cycles of planning, taking action and evaluating can be anticipated but cannot be designed or planned in detail in advance. The philosophy underlying action research is that the stated aims of the project lead to planning and implementing the first action, which is then evaluated. The second action cycle cannot be planned in detail until evaluation of the first action has taken place.

In Chapter 1 we described organization development as a collaborative, interventionist form of research, grounded in action research. Organization development engages in direct work with organizational members on the change issues that are needed (second-person practice). It demands that OD practitioners attend explicitly to their own learning in action (first-person practice). Second-person practice is primary in our view. It is through working with others while utilizing collaborative processes of engaging in co-constructing the project, co-planning action, taking shared action, engaging in shared evaluation and co-generating learning and knowledge that individual (first person) learning takes place and from that second and first experience and learning that change takes place and actionable knowledge (third-person practice) is co-generated.

We now return to Kevin and see how the three practices were at work in his project.

Box 2.2   The three practices

Kevin found the three practices very useful in his reflection on his experience. He realized that his main challenge was in how he himself would act as section head in the new setting, in showing a welcoming disposition to each individual and to questions being asked and thereby building a learning team in the context of the acquisition. Accordingly, he devoted a lot of space in his reflective journal to his own learning: that he was learning to cope with the pressure of being a change agent, how he dealt with criticism, especially when he thought it was unfair, and what he was learning about himself. This constituted his first-person work. His work with the current team marked his second-person work and he practised how to listen and to be patient by holding back on giving his opinions when he judged it better to invite opinions and to allow others to vent their anxieties. He also exercised second-person work in engaging with his manager and the other section heads by trying to model skills in being consultative and controlling his frustration. His third-person challenge was to write up his experience, link it to relevant literature and thereby present a dissertation to the university that would meet its requirements for a research document.

Questions for Reflection

Taking a reflective perspective, re-thinking Kevin's project, what seems to have worked well? What additional actions could Kevin have taken that had the potential of enhancing the three practices? Does Kevin's engagement in the three practices help you consider how they may be operative in your potential action research work? What might your first-person challenges be? What might your second-person challenges be? What might your third-person contribution to knowledge be? Write a reflection in your reflective journal on your provisional answers to these questions.

MODALITIES OF ACTION RESEARCH

Action research has come to be understood as a family of practices comprising action modalities. These modalities reflect the nuances adopted by different action research scholars to capture the particular emphases or context of their work. Table 2.4 provides a general summary of the most common modalities, such as: action learning, action science, appreciative inquiry, clinical inquiry/research, collaborative developmental action inquiry, collaborative management research, cooperative inquiry, intervention research, to name a selection.

- *Action learning*: Pedler and Burgoyne (2015) describe how action learning has traditionally been directed toward enabling professionals to learn and develop through engaging in reflecting on their experience as they seek to solve real-life problems in their own organizational settings.
- *Action science*: Smith (2015) describes how the key to action science is to be able to systemically analyse and document patterns of behaviours and the reasoning behind them in order to identify causal links so as to produce actionable knowledge, that is, theories for producing desired outcomes.

- *Appreciative inquiry*: Ludema and Fry (2008) introduce appreciative inquiry as a form of action research which focuses on building on what is already successful, rather than what is deficient, thus leveraging the generative capacity for transformational action.
- *Clinical inquiry/research*: Schein (2008) introduces clinical inquiry as where action researchers gain access to organizations at the organization's invitation in order to be helpful and intervene in order to enable change to occur.
- *Collaborative developmental action inquiry*: Torbert and Associates (2004) understand collaborative developmental action inquiry as a form of action science that builds on insights from developmental psychology, especially how leaders can understand their own developmental stages and thereby gain insight into their own action-logics as they work to transform their organizations.
- *Collaborative management research*: Shani and his colleagues (2008) define collaborative management research as an inquiry process whereby external researchers and members of the system collaborate on the study of an organizational issue through a joint project of deliberate change.
- *Cooperative inquiry*: Heron (1996) describes cooperative inquiry as where participants research a topic through their own experience of it in order to understand their world, to make sense of their life and develop new and creative ways of looking at things and learn how to act to change things they might want to change and find out how to do things better.
- *Intervention research*: Intervention research has emerged out of France through the work of David and Hatchuel (2008) and Savall and Zardet (2011) and is built on a detailed analysis of an organization's performance and the consequent development of management tools and actions to address deeply embedded problems.
- *Learning history*: A learning history is an action research approach in the from of a written document that seeks to capture the learning from a project, an initiative or event in a way that draws on the human experiences of those involved and emphasises a participative process that is devised to stimulate wider learning from those experiences (Bradbury et al., 2015). The aim of a learning history is to present an organization's story in a way that is true to the experience and that stimulates and informs conversation on what happened, why it happened and how future action may be improved (Kleiner and Roth, 1997).

While the array of these modalities may be confusing to you coming to action research for the first time, we emphasize that these different modalities are not mutually exclusive. They are sets of general principles and devices which were framed by action researchers to express their own theoretical emphases and their own practice. Each has its own emphasis and can be appropriately used in conjunction with other approaches. They can be adapted to different research issues and contexts. What is

Table 2.4 The essence and processes of action research modalities

	Essence	*Process*
Action learning	There can be no learning without action and no (sober and deliberate) action without learning.	Subjecting experience to questioning insight in the company of peers and taking action.
Action science	People are unaware of reasoning behind what they do.	Being able to systemically analyse reasoning and behaviour to identify causal links can produce actionable knowledge.
Appreciative inquiry	If people focus on what is valuable in what they do and try to work on how this may be built on, then it leverages the generative capacity to facilitate transformational action.	Working through 4 Ds cycles (Discovery, Dream, Design, Delivery).
Clinical inquiry/research	Researchers gain access to organizations at the organization's invitation in order to be helpful and intervene to enable change to occur.	Inquiring into organizational dynamics.
Collaborative developmental action inquiry	Learning to inquire and to act in a timely manner contains central and implicit frames that each person acts out of in given periods of time.	Inquiring-in-action by attending to action logics at stages of ego development and intentionally developing new ones.
Collaborative management research	Outsider researchers and insider researchers working together in learning about how the organization functions with the intent of improving performance of the system and adding to the broader body of knowledge in the field of management.	Using methods that are scientifically based, which are created or modified by the insider/outsider research team.
Cooperative inquiry	Participants work together in an inquiry group as co-researchers and co-subjects.	Group process in which each person is a *co-subject* in the experience phases by participating in the activities being researched, and a *co-researcher* in the reflection phases.
Intervention research	Combines a theoretical perspective and an intervention protocol in order to revise existing management theories-in-use and co-invent new models of collective action.	An inquiry process in which researchers focus on facilitating the experience of collective action 'from the inside' and thus have more direct access to and understanding of the issue.
Learning history	Capturing what individuals and groups have learned and presenting it through the jointly told tale enables readers to learn about organizational dynamics.	Presentation of history with multiple voices and inviting reader to learn from contradictory perspectives.

important is that you, as the action researcher, be helped to seek the method appropriate to your inquiry and situation.

In your dissertation, you may not be expected to demonstrate an intimate familiarity with the nuances of the thoughts of the major thinkers whose work is summarized in this chapter. Nevertheless, it is important that you are able to take an informed and knowledgeable position about the relationship in action research between knowledge and practice and, thereby, be articulate in grounding the nature of action research as a form of knowledge production. If you review Kevin's story and your reflections, you can catch an insight into how he framed his action research dissertation work in terms of both the action of the *core* project and the knowledge generation of the *dissertation* project. Within his MBA programme he was able to justify his decision to select action research as his approach as it would address both issues.

SUMMARY

In this chapter we have elaborated the foundations of action research. We have grounded action research in the realm of practical knowing, that is the knowing which is focused on practical concerns and which leads to improved actions. We located the enactment of action research in three practices: first, second and third person. Each of these plays a central role in your dissertation as you work with others to address the practical issues confronting your organization/department, learn about yourself as you enact the role of action researcher and generate and articulate knowledge that is solidly based in these two practices which is of use to others. We have shown how action research has many expressions or modalities, which provide insights into different ways of enacting action research.

3

COMPONENTS OF ACTION RESEARCH

INTRODUCTION

In this chapter we develop the idea introduced in Chapter 1 of action research integrating action and research in the service of addressing a real organizational issue and generating actionable knowledge. In Chapter 1 we located and grounded action research in the knowledge-practice debates, in organization development, a rich heritage of studying and changing organizations and in sociotechnical system and design thinking perspectives. In this chapter we apply the broad foundations of those chapters to framing what action research involves and we apply the definition provided in Chapter 1 to the *core* and *dissertation* action research project in terms of design and gaining access.

COMPONENTS OF ACTION RESEARCH

Action research has four core components: action, research, collaboration and reflexivity. The *action* is directed at addressing a real organizational issue, whether a problem to be solved or an opportunity to be exploited, what we called the clinical approach in Chapter 1. The *research* is directed to the scientific discovery process, by which we mean it contributes to practical knowing. The *collaborative* highlights the fundamental orientation that differentiates action research from traditional research in that in action research the research is *with* people rather than *on* or *for* them; what we introduced in Chapter 2 as second-person practice. Stakeholders in the research are understood to be co-researchers rather than subjects. Action research is *reflexive* in that by taking place in the present tense it requires a constant examination and evaluation of what is going on with a view to deciding what needs to happen next. This is the enactment of the cycles of action and reflection introduced in Chapter 1. A central contrast with traditional forms of research is that the action researcher is an agent of change, rather than a detached observer as in other research traditions. This chapter discusses these components as they need to be enacted in how you, as the action researcher, identify what is needed to engage in action research and explore key challenges of positioning action research in relation to the needs of the organization: a real issue, access and a contract. There needs to be a real organizational issue that the organization/department/unit needs and wants to address. The action researcher needs to have access to addressing that issue, either as the relevant manager or team member or as an external agent who is permitted to work on the project. There needs to be some clarity of the action researcher's role and a contract (formal and psychological) that the action researcher has access to the relevant operational activities and can ask questions which may be awkward or disturbing. As an action researcher you need to have a guiding conceptual framework to help initially sort out in a systematic way the system, its components and dynamics - the context within which the action research project will take place. Finally, as a part of taking action orientation, developing a design thinking mind set will help in the exploration of possible alternative structural configurations, processes and activities to aid in the implementation of the project.

CHARACTERISTICS OF ACTION RESEARCH

Gummesson (2000) lays out ten major characteristics of action research, each of which has implications for the design and execution of action research and for you as the action researcher. These characteristics develop our definition and discussion of action research in Chapter 1. We now discuss each in turn, showing how they were prevalent in Kevin's work. We pose questions out of them for your reflection.

Action Researchers Take Action

As an action researcher you are not merely observing something happening; you are actively working at making it happen or are engaged in changing the status quo. This is the realm of the *core* project introduced in Chapter 1. For instance, in operations management, the actions, for example, may be in the area of supply chain improvement or the development of a new product or service. In information systems, the actions, for example, may be in the area of experimenting with different ways to enhance creativity and innovation. In marketing, the actions might be the exploration of different marketing strategies. In accounting, the actions might be exploring the implementation of different reporting systems. In human resource management (HRM), the action might be exploring the implementations of different reward systems or different employee retention strategies or recruitment strategies or training and development challenges. What is central is that you as an action researcher in the *core* project play a role in the progress of the action towards its desired organizational outcome.

Questions for Reflection

What is the action in which you intend to engage in your action research work? In what business discipline is it located? In what business unit is it located? What is the geographical region of the system/unit? What are some of the potential key contextual elements that might be relevant to the action project that you envision? What is the intended outcome? In what relevant reading in this discipline might you engage to understand this context? Write a reflection on your provisional answers to these questions in your reflective journal.

Action Research Always Involves Two Goals

Action research always involves addressing a real issue and contributing to knowledge. These are the dual imperatives of action research. Action research is about research *in* action and does not accept the distinction between theory and practice of other research traditions. Hence the challenge for you as an action researcher is to engage in both taking action in the *core* project and contributing to its resolution, and standing back from the action and reflecting on it as it happens in order to contribute to the body of knowledge in the *dissertation* project.

Kevin's story reminds us of this dual focus.

Box 3.1   The dual focus

Kevin had two goals. As section head he had to take action. It was his job to build the new team and make it effective. He decided that preparing his current team to receive the incoming members was an important thing to do. In terms of his dissertation it would be the very actions of preparing his team that would constitute the *core* project into which he would engage in the *dissertation* project and make a contribution to knowledge on managing mergers.

> **Questions for Reflection**
>
> Standing back from Kevin's situation, have you a sense of the twin focus of your action research work? What is your *core* project? What is the specific challenge on which you would like to take action? Why is it critical for the system? What is your *dissertation* project? What kind of data might you want to collect? How might you collect the data while following a scientific proto-col? What might be its added value to the current body of knowledge? Write a working note on your provisional answers to these questions.

Action Research is Interactive

The central engagement of action research is what we called *second-person* practice in Chapter 2: working with people as co-researchers, exploring what the pertinent issues are, engaging in joint planning as to how to address them, tak-ing joint action, systematically evaluating what took place and articulating shared learning. Accordingly, the important second-person practice skills you need to have as an action researcher are relational, involving being able to build good working relationships, trust and cooperation, through being able to listen and be helpful. Schein (2009, 2013b; Schein and Schein, 2018) describes these skills as engaging in 'humble inquiry'. You need such relational skills in working with individuals, in teams and project groups, across the interdepartmental group and across organiza-tions and perhaps in inter-organizational settings, as Coghlan et al. (2016) describe.

Box 3.2   Interactive dynamics

Kevin's second-person work was very interactive as he worked with his team. He used the weekly team meeting to create a safe psychological space for his team to express their anxieties, vent frustration and focus on key issues such as HR, infor-mation systems and fears that they would be dominated by the incoming group and would lose their valued way of working. Kevin listened carefully and after everyone had spoken, invited the group to consider how they could address some of the prob-lems. He suggested that when the new colleagues arrived he would hold a similar meeting and that he would propose that small working groups of two or three staff members from both former organizations would take up particular issues and begin to draw up strategies as to how these issues might be addressed.

You also need to think as a designer as one who collaboratively crafts the structural configurations and processes that will enhance the inquiry process and the relationships between the collaborators.

We see these issues in Kevin's story.

Questions for Reflection

Who are the key stakeholders in your proposed action research work? Of these stakeholders who are those with whom you will be working directly and closely? What might they find intriguing and/or relevant? How might you engage them in the *core* and *dissertation* projects? How might they react to the emphasis on collaboration in the inquiry process? What might be the initial structural configurations and inquiry processes that you would want to explore with them? Write a reflection on your provisional answers to these questions in your reflective journal.

Action Research Aims at Developing Holistic Understanding

Action research aims at developing holistic understanding during a project and recognizing complexity. While a particular project may be located in one part of the organization or service and be focused on a challenge or problem within that area, as an action researcher you need to keep an eye on how that challenge or problem may be systemically linked to other problems or areas in the organization. You need to have a broad understanding of how the system works and be able to move between formal structural and technical subsystems and informal people subsystems. The sociotechnical system theory of organization and management can serve as a guiding conceptual framework that can help you develop a deeper level of understanding of the working system. As an adaptive complex system framework, the sociotechnical system can aid you in understanding the dynamic complexity arising from multiple causes and effects over time.

Kevin's story provides an illustration.

Box 3.3   Organizational context

While his primary focus was on the section of which he was the section head, Kevin needed also to attend to the broader organizational context in which his section was embedded. Accordingly, his participation in other organizational meetings – with

(Continued)

(Continued)

his own manager and at section heads' meetings – kept him grounded in the demands of the organization in its competitive market. He knew that he was not a free agent; he also had to respond to demands being made on him from higher management. When at the weekly meeting of section heads he raised the topic of integration in terms of the questions his team had posed, he received a mixed reaction. A couple of his colleagues dismissed his team's questions as 'They are only trying to avoid hard work'. The senior manager reiterated his demand for greater efficiencies and for the need for the new organization to be successful and wondered what the fuss was about. Kevin realized that he would have to manage his manager's and fellow section heads' perception of what he was doing.

Questions for Reflection

From Kevin's dilemma, what challenges are likely to come from the unit/ system context (i.e. wider organization, headquarters, other internal or external systems, competitive environment, regional dynamics)? What insights into how the organization works are likely to support and/or hinder your project? What might be some of the current structural and process configurations that could be utilized as inquiry and dialogue mechanisms that can enhance the project? Write a reflection on your provisional answers to these questions in your reflective journal.

Action Research is Fundamentally about Change and its Management

Mitki et al. (2000) classify change programmes into three categories: limited, focused or holistic. *Limited* change programmes are aimed at addressing a specific problem, such as team building or communication improvement. It is likely that such projects may be appropriate outlets for action research for MBA or other masters-level students. *Focused* change programmes are ones that identify a few key aspects, such as time, quality, customer value, and then use these, by design, as levers for changing the organization system-wide. This type is also likely to be attractive for action research for MBA and other masters programmes. *Holistic* change programmes are aimed by design to address simultaneously all (or most) aspects of the organization. These tend to extend over a longer period of time than the other two forms and are unlikely to fit the limited scope of a masters dissertation. However, an individual masters action research project may be a limited or focused change within a holistic one. We will see this in the example of Talia's action research project in Chapter 4 in Boxes 4.1–4.8.

As Beckhard and Harris (1987) demonstrate, you need to know how an organization recognizes the need for change, articulates a desired outcome from the change and actively plans and implements how to achieve that desired future. You also need to have a sense of how change moves through a system. For instance, Coghlan et al. (2016) discuss how organizational change involves individuals changing, teams changing, the coordination of work and processes between teams changing so that the organization in its engagement with its external world changes. Such change processes across individuals, teams, the interdepartmental group and the organization occur over time and are characterized by reactions of denying, dodging, doing and sustaining by individuals, teams and the interdepartmental group as the change moves iteratively between individuals and teams. Buchanan and Badham (2008) show how to be sensitive to the dynamics of organizational power and politics. A wide variety of planned change orientations can be found in the field of organization development, each of which can provide a conceptual guide for thinking about, designing and implementing change and development projects.

Kevin's project was about change.

Action Research Requires an Understanding of the Ethical Framework, Values and Norms Within Which it is Used

In action research, ethics involves authentic collaborative relationships between you, the action researcher and members of the organization as to how they understand the process and take significant action. Values and norms that flow from such ethical principles typically focus on how you work with the members of the organization.

Box 3.4   Organizational change

Kevin was clearly leading change. It was a limited change, namely preparing to build an integrated team within his section whereby each of the former separate organizations would have to change their thinking and ways of working to accommodate the new organizational setting. This limited change in Kevin's section was part of a holistic change occurring at the organizational level and Kevin had to attend to that process and be political in his engagement with senior management.

Questions for Reflection

Is your action research project limited or focused in its intent? Does the project occur within a broader, longer-term holistic change initiative? Can you frame the limit or focus of your proposed work? Can you envision a planned change programme with specific phases and activities? What are some of the change mechanisms that might be relevant to this project? What is the guiding conceptual planned change process framework that makes sense for you to utilize, such that you have an initial blueprint for the change process and phases? What are you hoping to change: structures, procedures, processes, ways of thinking ... ? Write a reflection on your provisional answers to these questions in your reflective journal.

You treat people as persons, and not as mere data points or research subjects. Accordingly, as you work with them on identifying pertinent issues for research and action and engage in the cycles of constructing, planning action, taking action and evaluating action, introduced in Chapter 1, you are engaging in ethical behaviour.

Actions taken have a direct and indirect impact on the roles, responsibilities, accountabilities and actionabilities of people and so cannot be treated without ethical considerations. Ethical dilemmas arise both in the imbalance of power in the organization and in the action research process of influencing by persuasion. We suggest that you keep two questions and four principles in mind as you enact the action research cycles. The two questions are: i) Who will be affected? ii) How will they be affected? The four principles are: i) Serve the good of the whole; ii) Treat others as you would like them to treat you; iii) Respect their being and never use them for their ability – in other words, treat people as persons and never as research subjects or data points; iv) Act so as not to increase power by more powerful stakeholders over less powerful. At its core, ethical action research involves genuine collaborative relationships between you, as the action researcher, and the members of the organization as to how they understand the process, plan, take and evaluate significant action.

The process of coming to identify values and making decisions based on those values is the first-person method we introduced in Chapter 2. You experience a situation. Using your sensitivity, imagination and intelligence, you seek to answer the question for understanding as to what the possible courses of action might be. At this level you ask what courses of action are open to you and you review options, weigh choices and decide. You reflect on the possible value judgements as to what is good or worthwhile or is the best option and you decide to follow through your value judgement and you take responsibility for consistency between your knowing and your actions.

Values were central to Kevin's thinking.

Box 3.5   Values and ethics

Kevin was aware that his personal value system directed him to treat the members of his team with respect. That was the way he had been brought up. Accordingly, as the section head leading the change he wanted to treat the members of his team equally and respectfully. He wanted to give each one an equal voice and to foster an open questioning climate where questions and opinions would be valued and heard. This wouldn't be easy as pressure mounted and anxieties grew and inhibited that open climate. He wrote a lot in his reflective journal about his efforts to remain calm and empathic towards the anxieties and struggles of his team. He was also aware that when writing his dissertation he could not write disparagingly about individuals, such as attributing blame or branding them as resistant. This would violate both his own values and the ethical principles underpinning action research. This was to be research *with* his team not research *on* or *about* them.

Questions for Reflection

What are your values about engaging in leading people in a change? How have you chosen these values? How might you enact these values, particularly in a political environment where the pressure may be on getting the job done, perhaps at the expense of the people? Have you identified the people that might be affected by the change? How might they be affected? What might be specific courses of action to mitigate the impact of the change on them? Write a reflection on your provisional answers to these questions in your reflective journal.

Seeking Ethics Approval

In places where research is conducted with 'human subjects' by members of an organization, whether by practitioners, researchers, academic staff or post-graduate students, the process for ethics approval can involve a detailed written application from the primary researcher, which is first checked and endorsed by an academic supervisor, head of department or research director, before being sent on to the relevant ethics committee. Engagement in the action research process involving 'human subjects' may not be permitted to commence until formal written approval has been received and this may take several weeks or months depending on whether additional information or amendments are required. This timescale will need to be managed as the *core* action research project may be working off a timetable that conflicts with the ethics approval process of the *dissertation* project.

Some institutions and universities have streamlined procedures for the ethical approval of research which is of negligible or low risk, with definitions and checklists used to assess the classification of a particular project. Factors taken into consideration can include aspects such as if participants are potentially identifiable, if they may be more vulnerable than average adults, and whether the researcher intends to ask sensitive questions, manipulate a stimulus or use deception. Many action research projects may be categorized as low risk where there is no risk above the everyday as the activities involved are part of normal business in the organization. Indeed, in some settings ethics approval is not required for action research projects as the system considers action research work as a form of project management, and not research. This is not a position that action research wants to be in.

Standard university, professional body and organizational ethics procedures and proformas are often based on the assumption that the researcher will be able to state in advance in some detail who will be included in the sample, what they will be asked to do, and when and where this will occur. While this approach may sit well with what would normally be expected to be able to be included in a 'contractual' agreement, it may not adequately cover action research projects which have a more iterative, collaborative, participative emergent approach. Standard proformas also do not normally require discussion of ethical aspects of the risks for the researcher. Since standard ethical approval procedures may not require researchers to explain how they will address these issues, researchers and their academic supervisors may neglect to consider and prepare for these possibilities, and as a result face greater difficulties and dilemmas than necessary when these could have been avoided or reduced.

Ethical considerations involved in the design of an action research project, as well as a formal ethics application, if required, include the examination of issues associated with perceived bias and coercion. Potential sources of bias can be related to what the researcher sees and asks, what participants think the researcher wants to hear, and what participants choose to emphasize, include and exclude. These issues are present in projects where the researcher is external to the organization but may operate differently in insider action research because of role duality. It is important to note that while ongoing working relationships may be associated with coercion or compliance, there are also authentic positive ongoing working relationships which can enhance cooperation and promote genuine collaboration. Action research projects are often already occurring in the workplace as part of normal quality assurance processes, innovation and change programmes, or everyday management processes. Accordingly, the applicant for ethics approval is not requesting approval for the *core* project to proceed. That is the remit of senior management. What is being sought in an ethics approval application is permission to use the data to write up the story as your *dissertation* project. The additional dialogue, reflection and rigour added as part of an action research project can improve the careful consideration of ethical issues in the process as well as the value of the outcomes for individuals and organizations.

Questions for Reflection

If you are seeking ethical approval for your *dissertation* project, what might the core concerns of the ethics approval board be? How might you show the board how you are dealing with issues of who will be affected and how? How do you intend to deal with consent and confidentiality? What is your strategy for dealing with unexpected events, such as if conflicts emerge or if individuals' apparent incompetence surfaces? Write a reflection on your provisional answers to these questions in your reflective journal.

Action Research can Include all Types of Data Gathering Methods

Action research does not exclude the use of a variety of data-gathering methods from the traditional research tradition. Accordingly, you may draw on qualitative and quantitative tools, such as interviews and surveys, as a means of collecting new information or consolidating information you already have. However, you need to realize that data collection tools are themselves interventions and they generate data. For example, a survey or an interview may generate feelings of anxiety, suspicion, apathy and hostility or create expectations in a workforce. For instance, a low survey return, while it may raise questions about the validity of the data collected, may uncover a suspicion about the survey or the project, which, for you as the action researcher, is useful, if not critical, information. If you do not attend to this and focus only on the collection of data, you may miss significant data that may be critical to the success of the project, or that may confound the data you think that you are gathering. What is important, then, in action research is that you collaborate with members of the system both in the exploration of the alternative data collection methods and in making the choice about what data collection method to use. In some projects the co-development of the data collection tools might provide added value. One can also explore the potential involvement of members of the organization in the data collection and in the data interpretation (sense-making) processes.

Questions for Reflection

How might data collection tools, such as a survey, focus groups, interviews or observations, be relevant and useful for your action research project? What might be the advantages and shortcomings of each? Whom should you get involved in the comparative exploration of the data collection methods and processes? What might the side-effects of the use of these tools be? With whom and how might decisions be made in regard to the data collection tools and processes? Write a reflection on your provisional answers to these questions in your reflective journal.

Action Research Requires a Breadth of Preunderstanding

Action research requires a breadth of preunderstanding of the external and internal contexts. Preunderstanding refers to the knowledge that you bring to the research project. As we introduced in Chapter 1, you, therefore, need to have a broad knowledge of the organization, its business context, its internal dynamics – formal, technical and informal. Such contextual knowledge is critical to the *core* project. In Chapter 1 we introduced the sociotechnical system framework. Such a framework can be used to help you capture your preunderstanding of the system and can also help you identify some of your knowledge gaps. You also need to have some familiarity with the academic context – what knowledge exists about the business environment and the topic that you are addressing in the *dissertation* project. As such, an initial exploration of the scientific literature about the potential topics is likely to provide some additional insights about how you can make a difference within the system.

Questions for Reflection

If you are an outsider to the organizational setting, what knowledge do you have about the industry, the firm and the particular field or topic in which you will engage? How reliable is that knowledge? Can you carry out a sociotechnical system analysis of the system based on the knowledge that you have? What are some of your knowledge gaps? If you are an insider, what do you know about how the system really works: where the points of influence are, who the key players are for your project and where the potential minefields might be? Can you carry out a sociotechnical system analysis of the system based on the knowledge that you have? What are some of your knowledge gaps? Write a reflection on your provisional answers to these questions in your reflective journal.

Action Research Should be Conducted in Real Time

Action research is research on a real issue (not one created for the sake of the dissertation) with those who are directly concerned with that issue and can address it. As Coghlan and Shani (2017) explore, an added dimension is that it involves researching in the present tense. As we noted in Chapter 2, much of what we refer to as qualitative research, such as case studies, is focused on the past. Action research builds on the past and takes place in the present with a view to shaping the future. Accordingly, as you engage in the cycles of action and reflection you need to be attentive and questioning as to what is going on at any given moment, be intelligent and reasonable in how you frame your understanding and how that understanding shapes your interventions and leads to purposeful action.

Kevin's project was in real time.

Box 3.6   Real time

For Kevin, preparing for the arrival of the new team members and the start of the new organization was real and had a time frame. The stakes were real and would have consequences for the organization and his section if not managed properly. It was in this context that Kevin had to act promptly and judiciously. He had to attend to what his current team members were thinking and feeling and he had to respond to that in the present as he worked to lead them to prepare for the change that would take place in a few weeks' time.

Questions for Reflection

What is your time frame for completing the task of the *core* project and for submitting your dissertation for the *dissertation* project? Where are interim deadlines and pressure points? What seems to be the time orientation of the system/unit? How would your time constraints work with those of the system? What might be some of the issues that emerge at different phases of the project, as the study progresses? How might you handle them? Write a reflection on your provisional answers to these questions in your reflective journal.

The Action Research Paradigm Requires its own Quality Criteria

Action research should not be judged by the criteria of other research approaches, but rather within the criteria of its own terms. The contribution of action research to the knowledge production discourse is not a matter of sticking to the rigour-relevance polarity of traditional research but of focusing on vital arguments relating to action, research, collaboration and reflexivity.

As with all approaches to rigorous inquiry, the action research paradigm requires its own quality criteria, taking quality to mean a grade of excellence. Eden and Huxham (1996/2016) provide 12 contentions of what constitutes good action research. These reflect the intentionality of the researcher to change an organization, that the project has some implications beyond those involved directly in it and that the project has an explicit aim to elaborate or develop theory as well as to be useful to the organization. Theory must inform the design and development of the actions. Eden and Huxham place great emphasis on the enactment of the action research cycles, in which systematic method and orderliness are required in reflecting on the outcomes of each cycle and the design of the subsequent cycles. Table 3.1 summarizes these contentions and offers guidance for your masters dissertation.

Table 3.1 Eden and Huxham's 12 contentions for a masters action research

Eden and Huxham's 12 contentions	Application to masters dissertation
Action research must have some implications and inform other contexts.	Be explicit about your *dissertation* project contribution.
Action research demands an explicit concern with theory.	Make links to reading and theory contribution.
The contribution of tools, techniques, etc. is not sufficient. The basis for their design must be explicit and related to the theory.	Link your dissertation project to a potential contribution to theory.
Action research generates emergent theory.	You will not know your theory contribution until later in the project.
Theory building is incremental, moving from the particular to the general in small steps.	Catch the small learning that occurs in the present tense as the project progresses via your journal notes.
Presenters of action research must be clear about what they expect the reader to take from it, and present with a form and style appropriate to this aim.	Don't merely describe what happened but point the reader to the emerging learning and added value to theory.
High degree of method and orderliness required in reflecting about the emerging research content of each episode of involvement in the organization.	Pay careful attention to overall project design configurations, the development of data collection methods and the inquiry process such that you can demonstrate the rigour of your methods.
Process of exploration of the data in detecting emergent theories must be either replicable or demonstrable through argument or analysis.	Show how you inquired in the present tense and how you processed insights so readers may understand what was going on.

Eden and Huxhams 12 contentions	Application to masters dissertation
Adhering to the eight contentions above is a necessary but not sufficient condition for the validity of action research.	Have a solid argument for how your action research is of quality that is embedded in solid theoretical foundation, inquiry and action.
Justify the use of action research by showing aspects that other research approaches cannot capture. Show your knowledge about, and skills to apply, method and analysis procedures for collecting and exploring rich data.	Show how your action research process is contributing to both the action and to theory in a way that other methods cannot do. Show your skills in the design of the project and the collaborative relationship building, intervention and reflection/analysis.
Triangulation is dialectical.	Be explicit about contradicting data.
The context for intervention is critical to the interpretation and applicability of the result.	Show how you know the context via the utilization or adaptive system theory or sociotechnical system theory of organization.

Pasmore et al. (2008) postulate that action research needs to be *rigorous, reflective* and *relevant*. *Rigorous* in action research typically refers to how data are generated, gathered, explored and evaluated, how events are questioned and interpreted through multiple action research cycles. *Reflective* refers to the attentiveness to the actions and the thinking behind them and the critical questions posed. As introduced in Chapter 2, action research takes place in the present tense and therefore is full of choices. As an action researcher you need to be aware of the choices you face as the project unfolds and make them clear and transparent to yourself, to those with whom you are engaging in inquiry and to those to whom you present your research in writing or in presentations. In this regard, keeping a reflective journal is essential as in it you can record your thinking at particular times and how you were reflecting on particular issues, how you were interpreting them and what decisions you were making at the time. *Relevant* refers to how the *core* project of working on a real issue shapes the *dissertation* project and challenges the inquiry to remain grounded in the actual demands of the *core* project. The explicit attention given to these questions and to the issues of being rigorous, reflective and relevant, and to the quality of the collaboration takes your action research beyond the mere narration of events to rigorous and critical questioning of experience, leading to actionable knowledge for both scholarly and practitioner communities. We will elaborate on Pasmore, Woodman and Simmons' quality criteria in Chapter 4 and will apply them at seven critical control (process choice) points. As an action researcher, you need to be clear how your action research work, particularly the *dissertation* project, may be judged to be quality action research.

An essential way of demonstrating the quality of your work, particularly in your first-person practice of being rigorous, reflective and relevant, is showing how you are following the general empirical method introduced in Chapter 2. As we described, this method is grounded in the basic activities of human knowing: being attentive to (experience), exploring intelligently to envisage possible explanations of that data (understanding), judging soundly, preferring as probable or certain the explanations that provide the best account for the data (judgement) and being responsible for your decisions and actions. When, as an action researcher, you attend to organizational experiences, converse with others to understand, and construct shared meanings (however provisional) from which appropriate interventions may be selected and implemented, you are enacting a general empirical method. In this manner you are embodying rigour in a science of action and seeking to address explicitly the pitfalls of working from untested inferences and attributions. The general empirical method applied to your first-person practice involves attending to learning how you learn through catching how, for example, you might jump to conclusions without sufficient evidence or how you might identify biases or be closed to certain areas of learning about yourself. It applies to your second-person practice as you engage in collaborative work with others and you learn about your skills in listening and team working.

In keeping with our definition and key areas of action research introduced in Chapters 1 and 2, we propose that quality in action research may be framed in terms of: purpose and rationale for action and inquiry, context, methodology and method of inquiry, design, narrative and outcomes, reflection on the narrative in the light of the experience and the theory; extrapolation to a broader context and articulation of actionable knowledge as are presented in the terms of their essence and are juxtaposed in terms of being rigorous, reflective and relevant as enacted through the general empirical method. We will apply this specifically in Chapter 4.

Kevin confronted the challenge of the quality of his action research.

Box 3.7   Quality

Kevin had to ensure that his dissertation would meet the academic requirements for his degree and accordingly he worked to be explicit as to how his account of and reflection on his work with his team would meet the quality requirements of being rigorous, reflective and relevant. In his MBA dissertation he showed how his *core* project was grounded in the challenge of integrating two teams from separate organizations into one. In his *dissertation* project he located it in how the literature on mergers and acquisitions shows that many fail because of the lack of cultural integration. So he had the practical and academic contexts of his work firmly established. He worked at creating an atmosphere in his team where team members could discuss their apprehensions about the upcoming new situation and explore together how to work through their fears and then engage with their new colleagues when they arrived. Thus, Kevin could demonstrate a quality of working relationship through the shared inquiry. Through the series of meetings where apprehensions were shared, and ways forward discussed and implemented in cycles of reflection and action, both the *core* and *dissertation* projects were advanced. The outcomes were that Kevin's team was ready to receive new colleagues and had a strategy for the integration of the two teams and new knowledge of how to approach the merger of two teams in the context of an acquisition was articulated.

Questions for Reflection

Learning from Kevin's focus on ensuring the quality of his work, can you frame the quality of your proposed action research work in terms of its context, the quality of working relationships, the quality of how the cycles of action and reflection are enacted, and the dual outcomes? What action plans do you have to address issues associated with the project's rigour, reflectiveness and relevance? Can you apply Eden and Huxham's contentions from Table 3.1 to your proposed work? Write a reflection on your provisional answers to these questions in your reflective journal.

WHAT IS NEEDED BEFORE ENTERING INTO ACTION RESEARCH

Before entering into your action research project, you need to position the proposed research in relation both to the needs of the organization or unit (the *core* project) and to the dissertation or research project (the *dissertation* project).

Positioning in Relation to the Needs of the Organization

Essentially, three things are needed to position your action research in relation to the needs of the organization: a real issue, access and a contract. A *real issue*, such as a process improvement, must be of managerial significance to the organization which is embarking on it, which has an uncertain outcome and which the group or organization is willing to subject to rigorous inquiry, particularly the analysis and implementation of action, and has research significance for you as the researcher. This is the *core* project which may be embarked on irrespective of whether or not it is being researched. Study of this issue cannot be carried out from a distance (or from the researcher's desk). Rather, you as the action researcher have to *gain physical access* to the area and to be contracted as an action researcher. This access may result from an invitation from the organization to your academic supervisor to help and your supervisor assigns you to the task. Alternatively, the access may result from you being in a position or role within the organization from which you can address the issues as part of your job. Developing the *contract*, a key element of the pre-step (outlined in Chapter 1), and execution of the contract require recognition of the different stakeholders of the issue, their differing expectations of interrelationships, processes and outcomes; interaction with the stakeholders in real time; data-gathering and data-generating opportunities; and confidence that they can be relied upon to engage in joint exploration of the issue. The stakeholders (or parties to this contract) include the key members of the organization who recognize the value of the action research approach and are willing (and, indeed, tolerant) to have the action researcher working with them through inquiring into the real issue, reflecting on it and generating shared insights as they progress towards workable solutions.

Box 3.8   Positioning for the core project

As a member of the organization and as section head, Kevin was well positioned to undertake the *core* project. He was tasked with making the new unit work in the context of the acquisition and he had access to the engagement with his team to prepare for the change.

Questions for Reflection

Have you identified a 'real' system issue on which you would like to take action? Do you have access to working on the issue in the organization, whether as an outsider or as an insider? Have you a contract to use this engagement for your dissertation? Can you explain the approach that you would like to take – action research – to the key organizational stakeholders? Can you explain why and how you judge action research to be the appropriate research to adopt and not other approaches? Can you explain the action research process and its key features to individuals who are likely to have a limited notion of what research or action research is and what researchers or action researchers do? Write a reflection on your provisional answers to these questions in your reflective journal.

Positioning in Relation to the Academic Research Education Programme

As we outlined above, your position as a masters-level student in an academic programme gives you the platform to assess your access as a researcher and the contract to study and write up the story of the core project. You need to have a sense of your potential contribution. We say 'sense' here deliberately as what you contribute may change as the project unfolds. Engaging your academic supervisor early on in the process is critical, just as is the parallel engagement with your superior at work. The academic supervisor provides the guidance – both in terms of meeting the academic institution's masters-level dissertation requirements and of the action research process.

Box 3.9   Positioning for the dissertation project

As a participant in the MBA programme, Kevin was well positioned to engage in the research. He had been exposed to a range of literature on mergers and acquisitions, on organizational change and development, on team working and on research methods and he had an academic supervisor to support and guide him.

Questions for Reflection

Are you familiar with the relevant literature and constructs in which your *dissertation* project is located and where it might develop? Can you provide a solid reasoning and be an advocate of action research to your supervisor about the merit of the proposed project and its methodological orientation? Have you a solid working relationship with your dissertation supervisor who understands action research and what you are aiming to achieve? Are you ready to sign an initial contract with your academic supervisor about the project, milestones, roles, design configuration, process, outcome and delivery? Write a reflection on your provisional answers to these questions in your reflective journal.

DESIGNING THE DISSERTATION PROJECT

The previous section opened up the positioning of the action research project in relation to the academic programme and the needs of the organization. As with any research, designing the *dissertation* project confronts you with challenges of framing the issue, determining its scope, gaining access and negotiating an appropriate role.

Framing the Dissertation Research Issue

In organizations there are many complex connections between inputs, transformations and outputs. There may appear to be a wide and diverse set of issues all vying for management attention. Some issues may be blatantly obvious, such as cost overruns, while others may go unnoticed, such as waste from inflexible response capability, unless attempts are made to uncover organizational members' perceptions of these core issues. Not every issue will volunteer itself automatically for resolution or, indeed, research. It is human construction that makes the difference, thus leading us to conclude that organizational actors' interpretations are pivotal in this whole process. Further, the organization may have framed the issue sufficiently to invite your academic supervisor to provide help.

Finally, the scale, scope and temporal nature of the core project may extend beyond the boundaries of a single dissertation research project and may even be supporting a number of dissertation researchers at the same time. So, framing and selecting the dissertation research issue from the *core* issue is a complex process that provides for some exciting opportunities for making a difference.

Determining the Scope

For you as the action researcher, the questions of who selects the scope of the dissertation project, who provides access and who is involved in it are important, as they are in any dissertation research. In this sense, determining the scope is through and part of an ongoing conversation, not just with the managers in the organization, but also with your academic supervisor or with the team members in a funded research project who may be engaged in their own dissertation research. It is in the conversation with your supervisor that the scope of your research should enable the identification of a phenomenon and replication of an intervention, perhaps in a new context.

Questions for Reflection

How have your earlier working notes laid the foundations for how you are thinking about your role and design? Write a reflection on your provisional answers to these questions in your reflective journal.

Gaining Access

Two types of access are relevant: primary and secondary. Primary access refers to the ability to get into the organization and to contract to undertake action research. Secondary access refers to access to specific areas within the organization or specific levels of information and activity.

Action researchers may play one of two roles in an action research project: outside agent and insider. The two roles are related but different. Sometimes, action researchers are outside agents who act as facilitators of the action and reflection within an organization. For some masters-level students, particularly those studying part-time, they are already consultants and their action research fits with their job. In this role, the action researcher is acting as an external helper, working in a facilitative manner to help the managers or staff to inquire into their own issues and create and implement solutions. As Schein (2009, 2013b) demonstrates, this role contrasts with the expert model as in the doctor-patient model where patients go to doctors for expert diagnosis and prescriptive direction. In this mode the expert solves the problem. In action research you are acting as the facilitator of inquiry and joint action. For others, the university or school may organize access to organizations as part of their ongoing relationship with some firms or the masters project may be an element within a larger research project.

There is also a growing incidence of action research being done from within organizations by insiders, as when practising managers, like Kevin, undertake action research projects in and on their own organizations. As Coghlan (2001) explores, this role is increasingly common in the context of managers participating in academic programmes. In such contexts the manager takes on the role of researcher in addition to their regular organizational roles and may both manage the project and study it at the same time. In this role, the insider action researcher should find access, both primary and secondary, easier. The other participants are likely to include subordinates and colleagues who need to buy in to the project. In addition, the manager is likely to have a personal stake in the outcome of the project. If you are an insider then your engagement in the action research involves you also paying attention to the challenges of your preunderstanding, role duality and managing organizational politics, as Coghlan and Brannick (2014) explore.

Negotiating a Role for the Action Researcher and Building Collaborative Relationships

In organizations, the typical focus is on delivering a product or service to today's customer, while considering also the possible requirements of tomorrow's customer. In that sense, the orientation is towards the task, the individual operators or managers, and the formal and informal systems which enable the individuals to carry out the task. What may not be so typical is reflection on the task and even inquiry into the learning opportunities derived from the task where the aim, priority, rationale, resourcing or achievement may be of interest. The reasons may be lack of time, of priority or even a concern about the political fallout from a review of practice and performance. In this context, the research takes on a challenging and even threatening character. As such, as the action researcher you may not be perceived as a friendly insider or outsider but as a threat to the status quo or to some vested interests. In addition, even if not a threat, the firm may not be able to distinguish research from consulting and, so, have very different expectations of a research-based engagement. This then is the world into which you as an aspiring action researcher step. Here, the invitation, if there is one, or the acceptance of an offer to research, may be associated with the development of an agenda for some individual or group and, so, expectations of the researcher may be set even before the first visit.

Roles are patterns of behaviour which individuals expect of others performing specific functions or tasks. As Coghlan and Shani (2005) discuss, there is potential role ambiguity and role conflict for any action researcher as different expectations of the organization and the university may make different and conflicting demands on the action researcher. Accordingly, negotiating a role whereby you as the action researcher can engage in the *dissertation* project, while engaging in the *core* project, is a necessary early step – and one to which you will need to return. Your role may be misunderstood. There may be conflict and ambiguity about what others see you as doing. In addition, the university may have its expectations of role. Further, there may be events or episodes which challenge the originally negotiated role and lead to re-negotiation. For example, there may be conflict between teams or departments which require a constant awareness of the atmosphere and an ability to re-align the role with change. How then do you as the action researcher deal with staff within the organization sharing their evaluations of their manager with an expectation of further dissemination or even action? The welcoming atmosphere in a meeting may change (due in no way to you) and lead to a ban on note-taking or any form of recording of comments. Such change compromises your role as a researcher and may lead to necessary re-negotiation. There is no assurance that the original role may be salvaged and, so, the research may end. Hence you need to manage politics astutely.

As we have stressed throughout the chapters thus far, action research is research *with* rather than *on* or *for* the organization. Within the organization, change projects of a strategic or operational nature may be ongoing in many domains of activity, and in parallel. One, some or all of these projects may be of interest or relevance to you as the action researcher. These projects may be directed by a senior management group which develops the focus and priority while deploying resources to implement the desired changes. Central to maintaining your researcher role is how you build collaborative relationships with these key members of the organization. This is the second-person practice introduced in Chapter 2. Within the organization you work with teams or groups of insiders that both own the core project issue or process and are engaged in new knowledge creation. In addition, you may work with a project steering group or other task force or team with a controlling interest in the project. In the core project, you participate in the steering group that is established by senior management and led by managers designated to be project leaders. These groups are essential for you as they drive the core project and provide you with valuable insider knowledge. Your role in such a group is to assist the group in advancing the assigned tasks. This is a subordinate role; you are not running this agenda and are not in control of it.

In contrast, in your role as the action researcher you may have a *dissertation* action research project group that can assist you in reflecting on the emerging insights, knowledge and learning. In your second-person practice with this latter group, you are the leader or convener; running this agenda and in control of it. The members need to be interested in the reflection and learning, be well connected across the organization and be persons of sound judgement.

Questions for Reflection

How are you negotiating your role as an action researcher? How would you negotiate the co-design of the action research project? Who might be the co-design collaborators? How are you clarifying expectations that you will be providing a learning process that will generate new actions, new insights and new organizational capabilities? How might you avoid being sucked into the organization's political games? Write a reflection on your provisional answers to these questions in your reflective journal.

DESIGNING AND MANAGING LEARNING MECHANISMS

The design thinking perspective presented in Chapter 1 advocates the need to purposefully design mechanisms that can enable action and reflection. Such mechanisms were labelled learning mechanisms, among other names. An important challenge in designing and implementing action research is the creation of learning mechanisms. As Lipshitz et al. (2002) define them, learning mechanisms typically refer to planned organizational structures and processes that encourage dynamic learning, particularly to enhance organizational capabilities. Most organizations tend to develop learning mechanisms in a natural way, although they rarely label them as such. Understanding the nature of the existing learning mechanisms is viewed as a part of the preunderstanding phase. Utilized well, the existing learning mechanisms can support the action research project in a variety of ways. As a part of the action research project, additional learning mechanisms can be designed as needed. The learning mechanisms provide an in-depth knowledge and understanding of the organization and as such can guide and support you as the action researcher. They embed the learning from the core project so that the organization maintains the benefits of the project in how the benefits are institutionalized in structures and procedures when the project is completed. They also act as reinforcing mechanisms so that the value of the core project is not dissipated once the energy has died down. The mechanisms can apply at individual, group, organizational or inter-organizational levels and can aim to initiate, facilitate, monitor and reward learning.

As Lipshitz et al. (2002) and Mitki et al. (2008) present, learning mechanisms are planned proactive features that enable and encourage organizational learning. Shani and Docherty (2003) identify three foci: *cognitive*, *structural* and *procedural*. *Cognitive* learning mechanisms are the cultural or cognitive mechanisms that are viewed as the bearers of language, concepts, symbols, theories, frameworks and values for thinking, reasoning and understanding consistent with the new capabilities. *Structural* learning mechanisms are organizational, physical, technical and work system infrastructures that encourage practice-based learning. These may include communication channels, the establishment of lateral structures to enable learning of new practice across various core organizational units; changes to the work organization, including the delineation of roles and the establishment of teams with shared accountability and thus a mutual need to learn; formal and informal joint exploration and debate, networks for mutual learning; and learning-specific structures such as parallel learning structures, bench-learning structures and process improvement teams. Finally, as Pavlovsky et al. (2001) describe, *procedural* learning mechanisms are viewed as the rules, routines, methods and tools that can be institutionalized in the organization to promote and support learning. These may include tests and assessment tools and methods, standard operating procedures, and methods for specific types of collective learning, such as action learning or de-briefing routines.

Most action research projects tend to create and implement a learning mechanism tapestry that includes variations of cognitive, structural and procedural mechanisms that promote and support action and learning. The challenge that you are likely to face is both in identifying what are the learning mechanisms that evolved in the system, figuring out how they can help in the action research process and identifying other learning mechanisms that you need to create. In some way, this suggests integrating both design thinking and learning into the action research project.

Questions for Reflection

What might be the alternative design configurations that can enhance action and reflection? Who might be the co-designers that will help you develop and explore the alternative design configurations? How might you build appropriate learning mechanisms into the design and implementation of your project? What might be an appropriate tapestry of cognitive, structural and procedural mechanisms? How would they enhance the implementation and inquiry process and outcomes? Write a reflection on your provisional answers to these questions in your reflective journal.

SUMMARY

In the first two chapters we introduced action research as integrating action and research in the service of addressing a real organizational issue and generating actionable knowledge, and located and grounded action research in the knowledge-practice debates, in sociotechnical systems as adaptive systems perspective, in design thinking and in organization development. In this chapter we apply the broad foundations of the chapters to framing what action research involves, the key characteristics of action research, differentiated between the *core* and *dissertation* action research projects in terms of design and gaining access.

This chapter captures the key characteristics of action research: action researchers take action; action research always involves two goals; action research is interactive; action research aims at developing holistic understanding; action research is fundamentally about change and its management; action research entails the design of learning mechanisms; action research requires an understanding of the ethical framework; action research can include all types of data-gathering methods; action research requires preunderstanding; action research is conducted in real time; and action research has its own quality criteria. The chapter also discussed the way to design the *dissertation* project and provided a blueprint for such endeavour that includes: framing the *dissertation* research issue; determining the scope; gaining access; negotiating a role for the action researcher and building collaborative relationships; and designing and managing learning mechanisms and learning mechanism tapestries. We invited you to engage in the clinical approach of asking critical questions - in applying the constructs of the chapter to your proposed action research - and articulating your insights.

4

ENACTING ACTION RESEARCH

INTRODUCTION

How do you engage in clinical inquiry as you design and enact your action research project so that the *core* project is successful and you make a theoretical contribution through the *dissertation* project? This chapter discusses how you might embark on and deliver an action research project for your dissertation. Here we build on the preceding chapters that introduced the philosophical and practical values of action, collaboration and reflexivity that underpin action research and how they may be realized by enacting the general empirical method through first- and second-person practice in the *core* and *dissertation* projects. The heart of the chapter lies in the enactment of seven core activities through which we now take you. As we take you through these seven activities, as in other chapters, we provide opportunities for you to take time to engage with the questions for study and answer them in your reflective journal. The *Questions for Reflection* are structured around a series of tables which direct you to build the quality requirements of being rigorous, reflective and relevant into your action research work from the outset. The tables provide a summary of the essence of each activity and the questions you need to be asking yourself to ensure that your engagement in each activity meets the standards of being rigorous, reflective and relevant. In this way you are building the evidence of how your experiences yielded insights, both about the progress of the project and about your own thinking, and how you tested those insights so as to affirm your judgements about your third-person contribution.

THE SEVEN CORE ACTIVITIES OF ACTION RESEARCH

The elements and characteristics of action research that we introduced in Chapters 1, 2 and 3, may be brought down to seven core activities. These may also form the basis for chapters in your dissertation, whether explicitly or not.

1. Grounding the purpose and a rationale of the research;
2. Describing the business, social and academic context of the research;
3. Articulating the methodology, methods and mechanisms of action;
4. Framing the issue to be addressed and the design to be followed;
5. Carrying out the action research process, capturing the narrative of what took place and its outcomes;
6. Reflecting on the narrative and outcomes;
7. Exploring how the particular situated action research project may be discussed and extrapolated to a theory-based context beyond that local situation, with perhaps a set of specific guidelines and criteria to enhance the overall quality of action research and how actionable knowledge may be articulated. You are expected to reflect on your own learning.

Purpose and Rationale of the Research

The starting point for action research is an issue (whether an opportunity or a problem) that needs to be addressed. It can be a strategic or an operational issue, a focused, limited or holistic change from which the imperative for action and for research follows. Kevin's case provided a clear illustration of how his dissertation was grounded in a real issue on which his company was embarking. When you are framing the purpose and rationale of your action research project, you are, in effect, presenting the case for action research, stating why the action chosen is worth doing for the organization (the *core* project), why it is worth studying and what it is that you seek to contribute to beyond the specifics of the project (the *dissertation* project). It is critical for you, as the action researcher, at the outset of your action research project, to make both a practical and an academic case for what you are doing and to declare your intention both to address the practical issue and to generate actionable knowledge. This is not just an argument for credibility but also a formal effort to locate your work in both practice and theory. You build up your picture by reading about your industry and its challenges and where your project fits within those challenges, and by talking to senior managers and specialists who can provide you with relevant information.

Your overall orientation and the demonstration of a comprehensive and systematic approach are critical. As we have discussed in Chapter 1, having a coherent conceptual framework of organization and management, coupled with design thinking, can help in the development of the argument and logic for the action research project.

Demonstrating that you understand systems, adaptive system complexity and the fact that you are also utilizing a design thinking orientation can help in generating legitimacy for you and the project that you propose. Placing the issue within the context of the need of the system and the opportunity to develop adaptable capability in order to continuously improve or enhance competitiveness is likely to be attractive to most decision makers. Advancing the basic collaborative design and design thinking logic that will guide the study also suggests that the system will be fully engaged in the study, where you might be the facilitator of learning by and with the system. It is not a study *on* the system, but as we stated throughout the book, it is a study *with* the system. Table 4.1 below captures the essence of the purpose of and rationale for the action research effort.

Table 4.1 Purpose and rationale

	The essence	Rigour	Reflective	Relevant
Purpose and rationale for action and inquiry	Describing why action and research are necessary or desirable, what contribution is intended, what the conceptual foundations are that guided the effort (hybrid of sociotechnical system, adaptive complex system and design thinking)	Does it provide a clear rationale for inquiry and action? To what extent does the focus address a gap in the scientific literature? Does it display the data to justify the purpose of and rationale for the study?	Is it linked to past research and scientific literature? Is it linked to contemporary business and organizational issues?	Does it describe why action is necessary or desirable (to achieve what for whom)?

Questions for Reflection

Table 4.1 poses questions as to how being rigorous, reflective and relevant are present in the presentation of the purpose and rationale of the action research project. Here are examples of the questions by which you may demonstrate rigour. Does it provide a clear rationale for inquiry and action? To what extent does the focus address a gap in the relevant management

(Continued)

(Continued)

and business literature? To what extent is the focus/issue embedded in a theoretical foundation (i.e. where would you place it within the context of the theoretical hybrid of the sociotechnical systems view of organization)? Does it display the data to justify the purpose and rationale for the study? Questions that ground reflectiveness could be: Is it linked to contemporary business and organizational issues? Is it linked to past research and academic literature? Questions for relevance could be: Does it describe why action is necessary or desirable? Does it require a focused, limited or holistic change? What does it intend to achieve and for whom? Write a reflection on your provisional answers to these questions in your reflective journal.

We now introduce the case of Talia and her action research work. Talia's situation is different from Kevin's. Kevin was a manager and his action research dissertation was undertaken from this insider position in the part-time MBA programme in which he was enrolled. In contrast, Talia was a full-time masters-level student and her action research dissertation work was as an outsider to the company and part of a larger research project that involved other researchers. Her story runs throughout this chapter.

Box 4.1   Introduction to Talia's project

Talia found the conversation about action research intriguing. She was finishing her first year of a masters-level programme in engineering management and was taking an elective course about management and the management of change. The professor was sharing with the class the early phase of an action research project that focused on creativity with a company in the fashion design industry. As she had to carry out a masters dissertation, Talia approached the professor and wanted to know if she could learn more about the project. She *was* fascinated by the inquiry approach, the industry and the topic. At the end of the conversation she asked if there was a way for her to join the project, to carry out her masters dissertation with it and if the professor would be willing to be her dissertation supervisor. Talia joined the research project team as a masters student that at that point in time included a senior researcher, a junior researcher and a doctoral student. The CEO welcomed the addition to the academic team and suggested that she would spend one day a week at the company, as a part of the project and her studies. The action research project moved into its second cycle with a clear focus on collective creativity.

The first phase of the study led to the realization that the real 'red and hot topic' of interest and relevance was not individual creativity (which was the focus for the first cycle) but collective creativity. Talia would be able to observe much more by spending one day a week in the company. She took on a comprehensive review of the literature on creativity and collective creativity. Many insights and knowledge gaps were identified in the literature. The dialogue in the study team – that served as a tapestry of learning mechanisms created to guide and lead the project and was composed of the academic research team and five individuals from the company – shifted the focus to begin the exploration of the meaning of collective creativity within the company.

Context

As we discussed in Chapters 1, 2 and 3, action research is localized and, accordingly, knowledge of and work within a context are central. Context here refers to the business, social and academic context of your research. There are three context areas: the broad general business context at global and national level; the local organizational/discipline context that is what is going on in your selected organization; and then the specific topic area. In action research framing the business and social context of the *core* project is very important. You need to do your reading on both the external and internal challenges in the relevant academic literature and in company documents. Therefore, you describe and analyse the context that describes the business context in which the organization operates, and the organization with which you are working. The sociotechnical system theoretical grounding, the adaptive complex systems perspective coupled with design thinking provide the conceptual framing for the description and initial analysis of the context and business dynamics. Your account of the context describes the external factors and elements that exist outside the boundary of the organization that have the potential to affect all or parts of the organization.

There are many ways of capturing the complexity of the external environment. The sociotechnical system perspective identified ten different sectors, each of which includes specific elements. For example, the industry sector (i.e. competitors, industry size and competitiveness, related industries), raw materials sector (i.e. suppliers, manufacturers, real estate), human resources sector (i.e. labour market, employment agencies, training schools), financial sector (i.e. stock markets, banks, private investors), technology sector (i.e. techniques of production, information technology, e-market), economic sector (i.e. unemployment rate, inflation rate, rate of investment), government sector (i.e. city, state, federal laws and regulations), sociocultural sector (i.e. age, values, beliefs, work ethics) and international sector (i.e. overseas markets, foreign customer, regulations).

The nature of the organization would entail factors and elements that exist within the boundary of the organization that have the potential to affect the organization functioning, dynamics and performance. Here as well, one can find many ways to capture the internal complexity of the organization. The sociotechnical system perspective presented three clusters, one of which is the external environment (described earlier), the others being the social and technological clusters. The interplay between the three clusters – via strategy, design, management systems and evolving culture – shapes the nature and performance of the organization.

As Pasmore (1988) describes, the social system cluster is comprised of the people who work in the organization and all that is human about their presence. It entails many elements such as individual attitudes and beliefs, the implicit psychological contracts between employees and the organization, and the relationships between working groups. The technological cluster consists of the tools, hardware, software, techniques, devices, artefacts, methods, procedures and many other elements that are used by organizational members to acquire inputs, convert input into outputs and/or provide services to customers, as instanced by Van Eijnatten et al. (2008). The design of the system that pulls together the environmental, social and technological elements, through joint optimization orientation, is concerned with the organization of the individual, group and task core processes through work structures and routines and management systems. Hanna (1988) and Taylor and Felten (1993) provide a rich account of studies on these issues.

This description of the system contains not only a presentation of the facts of the organization in its business and competitive setting but also contains a review of some of the relevant literature on the setting. The academic context (the *dissertation* project) is also important. Not only are you framing the business context of your project, you also need to review some of the research that has been done in that context and locate your action research in that tradition and so lay the ground for the hoped-for contribution that extends beyond the immediacy of the particular organizational setting and the people involved in the project, that is your third-person contribution. Table 4.2 below captures the essence of the action research context and its critical elements.

Table 4.2   Context

	The essence	*Rigour*	*Reflective*	*Relevant*
Context	Describing and analysing the business, organizational and academic context, while utilizing the hybrid of adaptive complex system, sociotechnical system and design thinking framework	Is the contextual data captured in a scientific, systematic and holistic way?	Does it build on past and present scientific research that is central to the focus of the study? Does it build on past and present organizational experience that is central to the issue studied?	To what extent are relevant analytical frameworks applied to understand the context?

Questions for Reflection

Table 4.2 poses questions as to how being rigorous, reflective and relevant are present in the presentation of the context of the project. A question for rigour would be, is the contextual data captured in a scientific, systematic and holistic way? Questions for reflectiveness would be, does it build on past and present research that is central to the focus of the study? Does it build on past and present organizational experience that is central to the issue studied? To what extent are relevant analytical frameworks applied to understand the context? Write a reflection on your provisional answers to these questions in your reflective journal.

We continue with Talia's story.

Box 4.2   The context of Talia's project

Based on the insights from the dialogue with the study team and what Talia was generating from the literature, the focus of the research became clearer. What constitutes collective creativity, what are some of the design implications for the formation and managing of collective creativity and how can collective creativity be measured became the central themes of the action research project. Talia co-led a presentation to the top management team about the emerging topic who gave its blessing to the study. It was viewed as 'mission critical'. She studied the nature of the industry, the history of the firm, particularly as a family-owned and managed company over four generations, how it had extended its business to China which had resulted in financial losses and how the board had hired an outsider as the first non-family member CEO. This new CEO had a strong background in finance and he handled, first and foremost, the financial emergency. He then formulated a strategic business development plan that centred both on efficiency and on improving customer service.

Methodology and Methods of Action and Inquiry

In your dissertation you will have to include a chapter on methodology in which the action research approach, methodology and methods of inquiry are described. This is a matter of providing some basic information on action research, such as was introduced in Chapters 1, 2 and 3, and introducing any particular modality (c.f. Chapter 2) that you are using. For example, if you draw on an appreciative inquiry modality, then you would provide a definition, some history and the main philosophical tenets of appreciative inquiry and justify it for this project. Alternatively, you may frame the action research as collaborative management research and so you would introduce this modality's tenets and methods and ground your work in this approach. You would also discuss the processes of first-, second- and third-person inquiry and practice and show how action research is an ethical engagement *with* people (second person) through which, by attending to your own thinking and evaluating through cycles of action and reflection in the present tense as the project unfolds (first person), you make a third-person contribution to the firm (in the *core* project) and to the literature (the *dissertation* project). You would also have to describe your methods of data generation and data analysis. Table 4.3 captures the essence of the methodology and methods of inquiry.

Table 4.3 Methodology and methods of inquiry

	The essence	*Rigour*	*Reflective*	*Relevant*
Methodology and methods of inquiry	Describing the methodology, the methods and process of inquiry, the role of the action researcher, the potential ethical issues, contracting process, the design and establishing of the learning mechanisms	To what extent is the process of contracting, selection of methods of action and inquiry collaborative? To what extent are alternative study designs explored? To what extent is the chosen study design described with sufficient details? To what extent are alternative methods and inquiry processes explored? To what extent are the chosen methods and inquiry process described with sufficient details? To what extent are alternative designs of learning mechanisms explored? To what extent is the chosen mechanism/s described with sufficient details? Are appropriate modes of action research selected and justified?	To what extent are the action and research cycles described? To what extent are learning mechanisms involved in the development of the methodology and inquiry method?	To what extent are the methods of action and inquiry driven by the organization's needs and scholarly criteria?

Questions for Reflection

Table 4.3 poses questions as to how the philosophical grounding of methodology and methods of inquiry build in structures of rigour, reflection and relevance. Possible questions to uncover rigour include: To what extent is the process of contracting, selection of methods of action and inquiry collaborative? To what extent are alternative study designs explored? To what extent is the chosen study design described with sufficient details? To what extent are alternative methods and inquiry processes explored? To what extent are the chosen methods and inquiry process described with sufficient details? To what extent are alternative learning mechanisms explored? To what extent is the chosen mechanism/s described with sufficient details? Are appropriate modalities of action research selected and justified? Reflectiveness may be uncovered by questions, such as: To what extent are the action and research cycles described? To what extent are learning mechanisms involved in the development of the methodology and inquiry method? Relevance may be demonstrated by answering a question such as: To what extent are the methods of action and inquiry driven by the organization's needs and scholarly criteria? Write a reflection on your provisional answers to these questions in your reflective journal.

We show how Talia engaged with the members of the firm.

Box 4.3 Talia's engagement with the firm

The study team – composed of the academic researchers, including Talia and the five members of the organization – explored different potential methodologies. After extended discussions it was agreed to use interview methods. The methods were presented by the study team to the top management who provided a few suggestions about the interview questions. The semi-structured interview guide was modified accordingly and sanctioned by top management. The vice-president for human resources, who was a member of the study team, sent an update email to all members of the organization and informed the organization about the next phase of the study. The interview protocols were developed by the study team – guided by both the experience in the company and the empirical research reported in the literature.

(Continued)

(Continued)

Twenty-one individuals were selected to be interviewed, using a purposeful sampling protocol, and the research teams conducted the interviews. The interviewees included: six managers from different levels and units; nine designers that represented different design teams, different length of experience with the company, diverse backgrounds; three sales people from different market segments; three individuals from different manufacturing units. Each interview lasted 60–90 minutes and was conducted by two members of the team. Talia co-led each interview. The interviews were transcribed and verified by both interviewers.

Design

Having introduced the context and action research, you now need to provide a general design plan and the utilization of learning mechanisms. Mapping existing learning mechanisms and identifying pathways for their utilization is needed. If you chose to supplement the existing learning mechanisms with some others or if you chose to design new learning mechanisms that address the need for cognitive, structural and procedural learning mechanisms, you will need to address both how they would aid in addressing the practical issue and generate knowledge and how you consider ethical issues. For example, your design might be built around project teams that would meet to address the issues confronting the organization and which might work in project management mode to structure addressing the issues. As the project proceeds in the present tense, you must also outline how you are dealing with the ethical issues of obtaining consent, ensuring anonymity and confidentiality and balancing conflicting and different interests in the cycles of planning, taking action and reflection. Your design needs to be informed by theory as well as by the exigencies of the situation.

The main source of data in action research is what is generated through the actions of the *core* project, such as in what people say and do (or do not say and do not do). As the action researcher you engage with them at formal project meetings and informally at coffee breaks and other occasions when they chat about the project. Your enactment of the general empirical method introduced in Chapter 2 (being attentive to this continual emergence of data, being intelligent in your understanding, being reasonable in your judgements and being responsible for your actions) is critical as it enables you to catch the data as it is being generated around you and to respond. If this data emerges during a meeting you can jot it down. If it comes through a conversation in an informal setting, such as in the canteen or through a chance meeting in a corridor, then you need to make a note as soon afterwards as you can. Later you will reflect on it in your journal.

In designing your approach to data generation you need to show how you are keeping an eye on the collaborative relationships. For example, you need to avoid giving advice as much as possible as giving advice tends not to build collaboration. Rather, you need to learn to ask questions that draw out others' opinions and ideas. In Chapter 2, under the heading of second-person practice, we introduced Schein's (2013b) three types of interventions: *pure, diagnostic* and *confrontive*. To remind you, *pure inquiry* is where you listen carefully and neutrally and prompt the elicitation and exploration of others' experience of the issues. *Diagnostic inquiry* is where you draw out others' understanding and interpretation of what is happening. *Confrontive inquiry* is where you move towards action by challenging others to think from a new perspective. As we emphasized in Chapter 2, Schein recommends that you spend a good deal of time in *pure* and *diagnostic* inquiry before getting to *confrontive* as the first two play a key role in building a mode of shared inquiry and shared understanding before getting to action. As Coghlan (2009) explores, using Schein's forms of inquiry is a practical format for using the general empirical method in working collaboratively in action research.

In some action research situations, particularly if you are part of a large project where there are teams of researchers, more traditional data collection approaches may be used. You saw this in Box 4.3 in Talia's case where she conducted interviews. While it may be useful to read more detailed accounts of how to design and conduct interviews, as presented by Cassell (2015), we provide an example of how such a common technique may be utilized in action research to show how you may conduct action research with reference to other books. Apart from demographic questions relating to participants' age and gender, Cassell (2015: 30-31) breaks interview questions down into four types that are used broadly sequentially as an interview proceeds. Firstly, there are opening questions which are general and uncontroversial. These are designed to help put the other person at ease by encouraging them to talk about something about which they have a lot to say. Answers to such questions may provide useful contextual information. Typical questions that are likely to work in an action research project include: 'How long have you been working here? What is your role?'

Secondly, there are what Cassell defines as other questions which are supplemented by the third type of question, which are the prompt questions. These two types of questions are the most important. The other questions are ones that are organized to address the research questions while the prompt questions encourage the research participant to expand on their answers. For example, the *core* project may be related to the introduction of team working into an organization. The *dissertation* project may be about whether participation in the design of change led employees to trust that the change would be positive. The other questions might be about the influence that employees see arising from participation, the preferred mechanisms for participation, the benefits that employees anticipate from teamwork, the obstacles that they see to realizing those benefits and the drawbacks that they perceive as arising from teamwork. Prompt questions may be derived from the academic literature asking about specific benefits and drawbacks arising from team working. Cassell's fourth type of question is the finishing questions and includes such invitations for the participant to add anything additional that they consider to be important but which the action researcher has failed to ask about.

As we saw in Box 4.3, the dual objectives associated with having a core project to realize goals involving change desired by the organization and a dissertation project that you have to write to satisfy the conditions of your degree programme, make it sensible and consistent with action research to have a study team to help inform the formulation of the interview schedule. It may be that you have defined your research question of whether participation in the design of change led to employees trusting that change would be positive by reference to the academic literature about trust in organizational change, as presented, for example, by Saunders et al. (2014). But as noted earlier, action research is not abstract; it is localized and context-specific. So you might seek to include the CEO or an assistant in the study team to help you formulate your interview questions in a way that is sensitive to the wider business context in which the company operates and its broader objectives within that context. Similarly, the intended introduction of team-working will lead to a change to the sociotechnical system existing at the organization, so you may seek to include the factory manager who can help ensure your interview questions reflect the objectives in the intended change. You might also seek to include your dissertation supervisor in the study team to help ensure that the research in which you are engaged continues to comply with the academic standards that will enable you to satisfy the requirements of your programme.

We would also encourage you to use such a study team when you analyse the data. For example, if you are using textual data, it may be that you want to use a form of thematic analysis such as template analysis, as outlined by King and Brookes (2017). King and Brookes illustrate how to prepare a template of primary, secondary and tertiary codes – or a hierarchy of headings and sub-headings – to enable you to organize the data to see the relationship between different components and dimensions of a phenomenon and which of those components and dimensions participants considered to be important. Including the CEO and the factory manager as members of the study team to design the initial template would help to ensure that consideration of the broader business context and the anticipated change in the sociotechnical system featured prominently in the codes. Including your dissertation supervisor in the study group would help to ensure that the analysis was organized to also address the academic literature.

We provide interviews and template analysis simply as examples. It may be that you and the organization require other forms of data and so other methods will be suitable, as will be evident as we proceed through the chapter. We would emphasize, however, that – as we have articulated earlier in the book – the essence of action research methodology is that the decision about the most appropriate data collection method, data analysis and data interpretation processes – the creation of meaning – is done in collaboration with members of the organization. The action researcher is viewed as both a research methods expert and, more importantly, as a facilitator of the co-discovery process, system learning and development.

You also need to keep in mind that data collection is also data generation. Everything you do is an intervention. While, for example, you may design and issue a survey to collect certain desirable information, you need to note that the questionnaire is an intervention into the system. While a low return may pose problems for the validity of the survey results, that low return may uncover apathy or suspicion toward the survey or the project. In this instance the significant data generated through the survey instrument is the apathy or suspicion in the organization and that is the data you may need to explore further and act on.

You also need to locate yourself in the project, i.e. as an external or internal facilitator or an internal senior or line manager. This is important first-person material. Here you introduce yourself in terms of your role regarding the project and position yourself and the challenges you face. If you are an external facilitator you need to explain how the research role was negotiated, especially if the initial contract was more oriented toward helping rather than towards research. If you are an insider you need to lay out how you deal with the challenges of your preunderstanding, combining your researcher role with your existing organizational roles and how you are managing organizational politics. You also need to portray the design of how you intend to engage in your first-person practice, for example keeping a reflective journal to capture your own thoughts, feelings and learnings as the project progresses and meeting your supervisor or mentor for consultation.

Your design may follow an established change design framework, as presented by Beckhard and Harris (1987) or Coghlan et al. (2016):

- Identify the need for change

This is your framing of the context, both outer and inner, and your case for why your project is needed.

- Build appropriate collaborative relationships

Here you map out the key relationships for your project: those you'll be working closely with and others whose support you will need, and how you intend to build quality collaborative relationships with them.

- Frame a desired outcome for the change

Framing a desired future or what things will be like when the project is completed is often neglected. This process is critical as it helps provide focus and energy because it describes the desires for the future in a positive light. On the other hand, an initial focus on the problematic or imperfect present may over-emphasize negative experiences and generate pessimism. Working at building consensus on a desired future is an important way of harnessing the political elements of the system.

• Develop a change plan and design the learning mechanisms collaboratively

Here a plan of action is devised. For the *core* project this may be led by the relevant manager or project leader. Regarding the *dissertation* project you need to have a plan as to how you will capture the data and structure the reflection processes.

• Implement the change plan and manage the transition

The critical task is to move from the present to the future and manage the intervening period of transition. This transition state between the present and the future is typically a difficult time because the past is found to be defective and no longer tenable and the new state has not yet come into being. So, in essence, the transition state is somewhat particular, as the old has gone and the new has not yet been realized, and so needs to be seen and managed as such.

• Reinforce and sustain the change through the learning mechanisms

Cognitive, structural and procedural mechanisms need to be established so that the change survives. Table 4.4 below captures the essence of the design elements, data collection methods and data analysis of the action research effort.

Table 4.4   Design

	The essence	Rigour	Reflective	Relevant
Design	Describing the collaborative data collection and generation, the cycles of action research and the building of relationships and engagement Describing the examination of the possible data collection methods, data analysis and data interpretation processes, the choices that were made and the rationale that guided the choices	To what extent is the project designed and implemented to ensure rigour? To what extent is the data collaboratively and rigorously generated, collected and explored?	To what extent is the project designed and implemented collaboratively? To what extent is attention paid to the development of the quality of the relationship?	To what extent is the research design directed to meet the organization's needs, as well as those of academic rigour?

We return to Kevin's story from Chapters 1, 2 and 3 as his story illustrates how he framed the project that he was leading as an organizational change.

Box 4.4   Kevin's roles

Kevin was both project leader and action researcher. The need for change was clear. His section would have an influx of new members from the other organization and a new culture would have to be built to support the overall merger of the two organizations. The desired future was a harmonious working of the new section and a minimal polarization of any 'them and us' thinking, particularly in his own current team, who would be remaining on familiar ground. The action research project for his MBA dissertation would focus on the first part, i.e. preparing his team for the arrival of the others. Clearly he would have further team working to do after the others had arrived but that would be later and outside of his MBA work. He developed a change plan of holding meetings with his team to specifically discuss the upcoming challenge and to prepare for the new situation. He wanted to create new thinking about the new situation as a cognitive learning mechanism and set up structural and procedural mechanisms to consolidate the new team setting when it occurred. He knew too that he would have to keep working at this challenge, long after the initial meetings so that the integration would be consolidated and would continue to work once things had settled down.

Questions for Reflection

Table 4.4 offers some questions to help you bring rigour, reflectiveness and relevance to the design of your project. For rigour you might ask: To what extent is the project designed and implemented to ensure rigour? To what extent is the data collaboratively and rigorously generated, collected and explored? To display reflectiveness, you might ask, to what extent is the project collaboratively designed and implemented? To what extent is attention paid to the development of the quality of the relationship? For relevance, to what extent is the research design directed to meet the organization's needs, as well as those of academic rigour? Write a reflection on your provisional answers to these questions in your reflective journal.

Here we show how Talia's role was defined and how she worked within it.

Box 4.5 Talia's role

Talia was introduced to the organization as a new intern for the next 6–9 months and would work out of the office of the vice-president for human resources. As a part of being an intern, Talia was identified as the liaison person around the creativity research project with the research team. The project was viewed as a part of her masters-level dissertation work. This was not an uncommon practice as the company was used to having masters-level students as interns. The study team that was created for the first cycle of the action research project was viewed as a structural learning mechanism. The academic research team, in the initial conversation with top management, suggested that one of the better ways to advance such a study was to utilize existing learning mechanisms and/or create new ones, as needed. The decision was made to use the top management team that met weekly as a steering committee for the project and to create a study team composed of the academic researchers and five members of the organization that collectively would be a microcosm of the organization. Talia began to cultivate working relationships with the different design teams, was invited to attend design team meetings and was a welcome colleague for many. She kept a detailed personal journal of the experiences that she had that focused on what was taking place in the company in general, thoughts about the research project, the new work relationships that were forming and personal reflections. Talia shared many of the personal reflections with the academic research team. These reflections and the dialogue around them guided the research team, as the team was progressing with the project.

Talia wrote in her reflective journal:

> Today I spend the first part of the morning preparing for the weekly meeting with the XY design team. The team has met three times since the project was launched and I joined the team in the third meeting that took place last week. I was introduced to the team by the team leader as one of the interns for the next six months and at this stage my task is to learn how they do things in the design teams. I was welcomed by everyone. A few key issues were raised during the meeting last week about the actual design of the tie that was a part of the collection for the XY age group. It seems like each member crafted her/his own design and the team leader kept the team talking about the different creations and their potential meaning. Three of the designs received verbal support from three individuals or more. Reflecting on the last meeting, my feeling was that people were frustrated with the process and the lack of agreement. It was not clear to me if they agreed to focus on the three designs and chose among them or if they could come up with a new design that was crafted on the spirit of the dialogue and people's

likes (to create some kind of a hybrid design). I am not sure if this is how this team works or if this was a one-time disagreement. It was clear to me that the team was experiencing conflict and instead of addressing it head on individuals continued to advocate for the design that they liked. A lot of emotions were exchanged but they seem to respect one another. It was also not clear to me how the team is making decisions and how they have moved from seven designs to three, but they seemed to feel good about the focus on the three. I guess I have a lot to learn about how this design team works, what some of the routines that they have developed are, what some of the norms, rules, rituals, decision-making processes, relationships with the team leader and among members and subgroup, and the like are. I am also not sure how they feel about me being present. They seem to respect me and did try to get my input on which design I liked the most. I chose to stay on the side line and said that I need more time to figure out what is going on but that I am really impressed by the great designs that they created. I was pushed a bit further and was asked which one I would buy for my partner. I felt that I was put in a box. At that point the team leader intervened and said that it is unfair to put me on the spot and that it is OK for me not to choose. I did not feel good about the encounter and am going to discuss it with my academic research team in our meeting tomorrow.

I may also need to develop an observation guide such that I can better capture the creative process in the team. I probably need to interview team members about the team, its processes of work, and get their insights about work and at the same time begin to generate ideas about what possibly can be improved. Maybe I also need to find a way to capture how the team worked and provide a few observations about what I have observed at the end of each meeting. A lot to talk about with my academic research team. Overall, I am concerned that the team has much to do. They have only seven weeks to complete the collection and prepare it for the transfer to production. I am not sure about the team and leadership dynamics, yet I was told that this team has generated great collections in the past. They better get their act together.

Narrative and Outcomes

The heart of any action research paper is the narrative or story of what took place. The story needs to follow intelligently through first- and second-person activities from i) the purpose and rationale as located in context, ii) the design as enacted through the cycles of action and reflection as a systematic method and order in constructing, planning action, taking action and reviewing outcomes and process and generating understanding, iii) reflections showing your use of the general empirical method as you moved through experiences, understandings, judgements and decisions, and iv) the outcomes for the firm. A critical issue for you in presenting the narrative is to distinguish the events which took place, about which there is no dispute, and the meanings you and relevant others attribute to these events. You provide an account of what took place in a factual and neutral manner. At the same time, during the project you will have identified and explored the different meanings and values attributed to particular events in the dialogues and conversations throughout the project. Your narrative needs to relate the differences and how they were discussed to what outcome. Your view of these events and your understanding and theorizing as to what these events are considered to mean should not be mixed in with the telling of the story. By separating the narrative from its interpretation, that is description from explanation, by clearly stating which is story and which is interpretation, you are demonstrating how you are applying methodological rigour to your approach. Combining narrative and interpretation leaves you open to the charge of biased storytelling and makes it difficult for readers and examiners to evaluate your work. Table 4.5 below captures the essence of the narrative and outcomes of action research initiative.

Table 4.5 Narrative and outcomes

	The essence	Rigour	Reflective	Relevant
Narrative and outcomes	Providing an account of the story and outcomes (intended and unintended)	How well is the story told, with an appropriate level of detail? To what extent are facts and values distinguished?	To what extent does the story demonstrate collaborative inquiry and action in the present tense?	To what extent does it capture what happened? What were the outcomes, both intended and unintended?

Questions for Reflection

The questions in Table 4.5 challenge the narrative of the events of the project in terms of being rigorous, reflective and relevant. For rigour you need to ask, how well is the story told, with an appropriate level of detail? To what extent are facts and values distinguished? For reflectiveness, to what extent does the story demonstrate collaborative inquiry and action in the present tense?

> For relevance, to what extent does it capture what happened? What were the outcomes, both intended and unintended? Write a reflection in your reflective journal that maps the flow of the actions and interpretations across both the *core* and the *dissertation* projects.

The following extract from Talia's story shows how her project progressed.

Box 4.6   Continuing Talia's account

Talia's journal captured the richness of the story of the second cycle of the action research project. It captured not only how the project evolved and what actually took place in detail, but also included encounters that she has had and company events in which she had participated. The journal reflection, as narrated above, included deeper-level insights on the challenges of establishing true collaborative inquiry. Many of the design teams had demonstrated success over time. They tended to develop a distinct sub-culture. They did not always welcome new people or outsiders. For example, Talia's unintended insight was that the five design teams in the women's division (each team specialized in designing collections for a specific age group) did not always share new ideas of either designs or new material across teams. When she began to question this practice, it triggered new conversations between the design team leaders. Beyond the initial denial of the emerging practice (or lack of), the team leaders acknowledged that some competition seemed to exist between the design teams. The conversation led to the agreement to explore different ways to share what is being learned and advanced across teams within the division.

Reflection on the Narrative and Outcomes

Having told the story of what took place to what effects, you need now to stand back and reflect and present your understanding of the events of the narrative and your understanding as to what these events and outcomes are considered to mean and what your judgements are about them. You judge the outcomes, both intended and unintended, desired and undesired, in terms of the intention of the project to address the organization's needs, whether as limited, focused or part of holistic change programmes. You need to draw on relevant literature on how change is successful or unsuccessful, for example Kotter (1995) or Pasmore (2011). You judge the collaborative processes as rigorous, reflective and relevant in coming to judgement about the project's success or otherwise. Table 4.6 captures elements of the reflections on the action research project story and outcomes.

Table 4.6   Reflection on the story and outcomes

	The essence	Rigour	Reflective	Relevant
Reflection on the story and outcomes	Analysing the story, reflection and critical judgements on the process and outcomes	To what extent do the narrative and description of the process and outcomes meet the standards/criteria of research?	To what extent is the story reflected on collaboratively? To what extent is shared meaning created? To what extent did dialogue about meaning and possible actions among different organizational groups/units/communities of practice take place?	To what extent are story and outcomes' meaning focused on the organization's needs? To what extent are story and outcomes' meaning focused on addressing scientific needs?

Questions for Reflection

Table 4.6 provides some questions to enable you to bring rigour, reflectiveness and relevance to your reflection on the narrative and outcomes. Under rigour you may ask, to what extent do the narrative and description of outcomes meet the standards and criteria of research? Under reflective to what extent is the story reflected on collaboratively? To what extent is shared meaning created? To what extent did dialogue about meaning and possible actions among different organizational groups/units/communities of practice take place? To demonstrate relevance you may ask, to what extent are story and outcomes' meaning focused on the organization's needs? To what extent are story and outcomes' meaning focused on addressing the needs of knowledge production? Write a reflection on your answers to these questions in your reflective journal.

Box 4.7   Continuing Talia's account

Talia played an important role in both the study and the company. Being driven by the appreciation for true collaboration Talia kept questioning the academic research team and the study team – 'are we collaborating enough?' In the short time that she was involved with the project she evolved to become a link not only between the research team members, the research team and the study team, and the study team and the organization, but also between individuals, teams and units within the organization.

Sense making was an important dimension of the project. Following the data collection phase, the study team devoted a significant amount of time to working through sense making. A 25-page document was created that captured raw statements around nine different categories. The content analysis of the data, while using sophisticated software and coding protocol, served as the bases for the content grouping and as the bases for the dialogue about meaning. The document that was generated was shared with the top management team that was asked to help in the further development of sense making. Talia suggested that they have an open session and invite organizational members to an organization ideas meeting to continue the process of sense making. After some discussion, the CEO offered to pay for coffee and pastries for such a meeting. The open invitation resulted in the attendance of 45 individuals and a very meaningful dialogue that was led by the study team. Following a brief introduction by the CEO, the study team provided an overview of the study to date and individuals were asked to join a round table for deeper-level conversation. Each table conversation was facilitated by a member of the study team. Following the sense making each table was asked to generate ideas for actions. The study team compiled all the ideas and generated a summary report that was shared with the top management team. The management team identified six areas for action and each member of the team was asked to be a champion for one action project and report to the group within six weeks about progress.

Discussion and Extrapolation to a Broader Context and the Articulation of Actionable Knowledge

A key issue that requires attention is that the action research study must have implications beyond the remit of the immediate project. In your dissertation this is likely to feature in your final chapter that captures your third-person practice. Action research projects are situation specific and do not always aim to create universal knowledge. At the same time, extrapolation from a local situation to more general situations is of utmost importance. You are not claiming that every organization will behave as the one you have studied. But you can focus on some significant factors, consideration of which is useful for other organizations, perhaps like organizations or organizations undergoing similar types of change processes, the application of a framework to a new context, or offer a contribution to methodology. Remember Eden and Huxham's (1996) point in Chapter 3 that the contribution of tools, techniques, etc. is not sufficient. The basis for their design must be explicit and related to the theory. In moving towards the final chapter of your dissertation, you reflect on the purpose and rationale for action and inquiry, the context, methodology, design and method of inquiry, narrative and outcomes, and demonstrate rigour, reflectiveness and relevance. Table 4.7 below captures the essence of the action research project discussion dimension.

Table 4.7 Discussion

	The essence	Rigour	Reflective	Relevant
Discussion and extrapolation to a broader context

Articulation of actionable knowledge | Articulating the links to theory (existing and emerging), deep level discussion of the story, the outcomes, the action research process, quality of relationships, sustainability of the outcomes and capturing the contribution to both theory and practice | To what extent does the entire account (purpose/ rationale, methodology and methods, design, narrative and outcomes, reflection, the quality of the action research process, the quality of relationships) contribute to knowledge and practice? | To what extent does the entire account (purpose/ rationale, methodology and methods, design, narrative, outcomes, sustainability of the outcomes and reflection) fit the quality of the action research process and the quality of relationships? | To what extent does the entire account (purpose/rationale, methodology and methods, design, narrative and outcomes, reflection) contribute to sustainable outcomes for the organization and actionable knowledge for scholars?

To what extent does the action research approach demonstrate returns that make the process and effort worthwhile? |

Questions for Reflection

The questions in Table 4.7 are aimed at focusing integration. What impact did context have on the project, especially if it changed or evolved in some way? How do you judge the quality of relationships between you as the action researcher and organizational members, and how were the relationships managed through trust, collaboration, dialogue concerns for one another's interest, equality of influence, common language and so on? What is your judgement on the quality of the action research process itself – how the collaborative processes of shared inquiry and action worked through the cycles of action and reflection in dealing with the challenges of the *core* project and in knowledge co-generation in the *dissertation* project? Finally, you reflect on the outcomes of the project – what might be sustainable (human, social, economic, ecological) through the learning mechanisms and competencies out of the action and the creation of knowledge from the inquiry? Write a reflection in your reflective journal on your provisional answers to these questions which will later form the core of the final chapter of your dissertation.

Finally, Talia's conclusions:

Box 4.8   Talia's conclusions

Talia's dissertation while focusing on collective creativity also highlighted the critical role that collaboration plays in action research, the essence of it, the difficulties in designing for it and the challenges of sustaining it in organizational life. She also explored the interplay between learning mechanisms and collective creativity. Talia stipulated that organizations probably need to explore the role that the tapestry of learning mechanisms which evolve in organizations that utilize action research plays in enhancing collaboration and collective creativity.

SUMMARY

This chapter has shown you how to design and enact your action research project and ensure that it meets the quality requirements of being rigorous, reflective and relevant. We have presented seven core activities: grounding the purpose and a rationale of the research; describing the business, social and academic context of the research; articulating the methodology, methods and mechanisms of action and inquiry; framing the issue to be addressed and the design to be followed; carrying out the action research process, capturing the narrative of what took place and its outcomes; reflecting on the narrative and outcomes and exploring how the particular situated action research project may be discussed and extrapolated to a context beyond that local situation and how actionable knowledge may be articulated. These seven activities provide a set of specific guidelines and criteria to enhance the overall quality of your action research project as rigorous, reflective and relevant. They may also provide a structure for the dissertation document that you will submit to your programme.

5

EXAMPLES OF ACTION RESEARCH

INTRODUCTION

The business and management literature provides many examples of action research implementation. The aim of this chapter is to present the wide range of action research projects that were impactful both in addressing specific organization issues and in advancing our understanding of business and management. To capture the wide range of action research implementations, we have grouped the examples by industry sector, business function or discipline, and insider action research emphasis.

CONTEXT

As we described in Chapter 1, the context in which action research is understood and conducted is central. The evolution of the action research approach as a research method of practice emerged within a wide variety of academic disciplines and contexts. In the first part of this chapter we discuss three contexts: industry sector, business disciplines and insider action research.

Industry sector

Over the years, action research has been utilized in a wide variety of industries, which include agriculture, biopharma, business and information, construction, education, energy, fashion design, food, defence, health care, automotive, telecommunication, fish farming, mining, pharmaceutical and public service. In this section we provide an illustration of action research studies that were conducted in eight industries: energy, manufacturing, media, merchant shipping, mining, food, health care and pharmaceutical.

Baker and Jayaraman (2012) describe a study in the *energy* industry where an action research project focused on the role of information processing and maintenance inventory in keeping the production process functioning and on schedule. The study resulted in the development of new process maps and cause-and-effect diagrams that contributed to a 27% reduction in inventory. Pace and Argona (1989) report on a participatory action research longitudinal project at a *manufacturing* division of Xerox Corporation. This project focused on the implementation of an experiential Quality of Working Life programme. The study reports with details the implementation process, phases, activities and mechanisms and some of the outcomes.

Meister and Gronski (2007) present an action research study in a virtual setting in a Canadian manufacturing company. The authors describe how the action research project evolved, some of the challenges in the facilitation of an action research project in a virtual setting and some of the reported outcomes in terms of process and improvements. An action research study with managers working for Danish press, radio and television organizations is described by Lund (2008). This study focused on change management in media business and offers a list of lessons for practical management in line with the three steps of applied action research: action, reflection and improvement. In the *merchant shipping* industry, Walton and Gaffney (1989) report on an action research study that focused on exploring a variety of strategies to promote organizational change in the Norwegian context. Through action research cycles of research and action, a wide range of changes were implemented. New conceptual framing with some specific guiding principles for industry-based action research studies was advanced.

Blumberg and Pringle (1983), in an action research study within the *mining* sector, focused on the Rushton Coal Mine to study how the use of control groups can lead to incomplete and erroneous data and sometimes to the project's termination. Several designs, which included adaptive experimental designs, were used to address an improvement in the dynamics and performance of the control groups. Kocher et al. (2011) generated detailed insights into the nature of innovation dynamics in the *food* industry and demonstrated how action research can be used to change and enhance SMEs' capability to innovate.

Shani and Eberhardt (1987) reported on an action research study in a *health care* institution. The action research project generated detailed insights into the creation of a supplemental structure – a parallel organization – that enhanced team effectiveness and performance. The study was led by a steering committee and a study group that, together, were viewed as a microcosm of the organization. Through a collaborative process, the study's scope, research methods (that included two surveys and two sets of semi-structured interviews) and process were developed and implemented by the parallel organization. Following the initial data sense making within the parallel organization and in collaboration with the management group of the hospital, the experimental design of teams was created and empirically studied. Based on the new insights that were generated, new team-based design principles were developed and the protocol for the new design was established to guide the system-wide design to be implemented. In addition, the study reports that new communication channels within and between the medical staff and administrative staff were established.

Finally, in the *pharmaceutical* industry, an action research approach was applied by Ngwerume and Themessl-Huber (2010) to develop a community pharmacy team, consisting of a pharmacist and medicine counter assistants, into a research-aware practice. The project contributed to the development of portfolios of evidence-based recommendations and scholarly insights.

Table 5.1 provides a synopsis of the selected studies briefly captured above. The examples reviewed above illustrate the utilization of action research in a wide variety of industry sectors, national and regional contexts. The examples demonstrate the various theoretical foundations that were used and the various and varied purposes for the efforts. The common denominators reflected in the studies seem to centre on the emphasis of individual and system engagement, the dual desired outcomes of system improvements and generation of scientific knowledge, the continuous action research cycles and phases and the learning mechanisms that were created to lead and guide the efforts.

Business functions/disciplines

As well as in industry sectors, action research has been utilized in various business functions/disciplines, which include accounting, e-marketing, e-commerce, e-learning, finance, information systems (IS/IT), lean operation management, management, consulting, customer service, marketing, human resource, research and development, manufacturing, purchasing, supply chain management, research and development, and sales to improve organizational efficiency. The *European Journal of Marketing* devoted a special issue to action research in 2004. In this section we feature illustrative examples from nine functions/disciplines: customer service, e-commerce, finance, human resource management, information systems, operation management, supply chain management, R&D, and marketing and e-marketing. This selection of the utilization of action research in the variety of business disciplines illustrates the drive to trigger and improve systems and simultaneously generate new scholarly insights about emerging challenges faced within and between the business disciplines.

Ballantyne (2004) undertook the study to provide an understanding of action research methodology in a marketing context in the light of uncertain knowledge

Table 5.1 Examples of action research in industry sectors: Brief synopsis

Industry sector	Authors, year	Purpose	Key features	Outcomes
Energy	Baker and Jayaraman, 2012	To investigate the important role that information processing and maintenance inventory play in keeping the production process functioning on schedule	Continuous cycles of action research of planning, action and evaluation Five phases of action research Rigorous scientific action research process	Facilitated the establishment of collaborative project teams Continuous review algorithm for inventory management system Documented improved profitability
Manufacturing	Pace and Argona, 1989	The project focused on the implementation of an experiential Quality of Working Life programme in a manufacturing division of Xerox Corporation	Union and management as trainers and coordinators Steering committee composed of management and union leaders Parallel problem-solving teams	Significant cost savings and productivity improvements Improvement in working conditions, work flow processes, quality and safety
Manufacturing	Meister and Gronski, 2007	To explore how action research might work in a virtual setting within a Canadian manufacturing company	Five-phased action research framework Research team included both internal and external members 10 virtual teams took part in the study All communications, data collection methods and data sense making were conducted electronically	Significant learning on how to conduct a virtual action research project Significant learning on virtual teams' dynamics and performance
Media – press, radio and television	Lund, 2008	Action research in a Danish media conglomerate for the purpose of innovations diffusion	Research team guided the action research project Four-phased action research framework	Specific sets of leadership qualities that enhance innovation diffusions were identified Design implications that enhance innovation diffusions were identified and implemented Significant improvement in innovation diffusion was recorded
Merchant shipping	Walton and Gaffney, 1989	Exploring a variety of strategies to promote organizational change in the Norwegian context	Five-phased action research cycles guided the PAR project Steering team, comprised of four union representatives, three government directors and three researchers, led the PAR project Study team composed of managers and seafarers guided the project within the company Committees composed of workers and managers carry out specific focused studies and experiments	Learning mechanisms that were viewed as innovations were diffused throughout the company and the industry Insights about the optimal number of seamen onboard were implemented – resulted in a significant reduction New work processes were implemented that improved productivity

Industry sector	Authors, year	Purpose	Key features	Outcomes
Mining	Blumberg and Pringle, 1983	Action research project with Rushton Coal Mine to study how the use of control groups can lead to incomplete and erroneous data and sometimes to the project's termination	Collaborative action research team led the project Collaborative research design led to design of a few controlled quasi-experiments Collaboration focused on evaluation criteria, outcomes measurement and processes	New roles of foremen as advisors, consultants, trainers and planners were developed Autonomous work teams-based organization was established Skill-based performance system was implemented Performance indicators demonstrated improvements in productivity, absenteeism, costs, health and safety matters
Food	Kocher et al., 2011	Action research project to generate detailed insights into the nature of innovation dynamics to change and enhance SMEs' capability to innovate in a Swiss food industry	Three sequential action research cycles Four action research phases were implemented within each action research cycle Research team guided the action research project	Insights are clustered in four levels: process, cultural, strategic and structural Changes that were implemented at the four levels resulted in new innovation capabilities, better diffusion of innovations and improved company performance
Health care	Shani and Eberhardt, 1987	Action research project generated detailed insights into the creation of a supplemental structure – a parallel organization – that enhanced team effectiveness and performance	A steering committee and a study group were established as a management advisory entity Through a collaborative process the study's scope, research methods and process were developed and implemented Following the initial findings, an experimental design of teams was created and empirically investigated	The parallel organization led the action research project New team-based design principles and protocol were established to guide the design of teams New communication channels within and between the medical staff and administrative staff were established
Pharmaceutical	Ngwerume and Themessl-Huber, 2010	Action research project to develop a community pharmacy team, consisting of a pharmacist and medicine counter assistants, into a research-aware practice	Cyclical action research process was utilized Four activity cycles, each of which involved representatives of the network, evolved during the project An evidence-based approach guided each phase of the action research project	Increased awareness of Medical Counter Assistance (MNCs) New research capacity and capability Improved customer-focused information system

of what was considered critical in *customer service* improvements. The study was conducted in a major retail bank and resulted in significant customer service improvements. A conclusion was reached that market-oriented action research was knowledge renewal achieved through an iterative process of action and learning. Daniel and Wilson (2004) report on how in *e-commerce* an action research study incorporated Directional Policy Matrix (DPM) to capture the competition between business models. The objectives of the study were to help participating organizations to prioritize their e-commerce projects using a method that could be generalized to and shared with other organizations and to synthesize the experience of using the method successfully.

Waddell (2012) conducted an action research project in *finance*. The project explored the role of action researchers as initiators of change by building on a Global Finance Initiative (GFI) experience and proposing an eight-step methodology. The case study indicated that conducting action research with large global systems was not simple and that it was critical to succinctly present the complexity to the stakeholders. Action research made a meaningful contribution of bringing discipline, rigour, insight and human connections to address a financial global system challenge. Lindgren et al. (2004) explored the role of information technology in managing *human resources* competence in six Swedish organizations. The authors use an action research approach to develop and test design principles for competence management systems. In addition to developing a set of design principles and considering their implications for both research and practice, this study includes a self-assessment while utilizing the criteria for canonical action research. Avital (2005) conducted an action research study within the *information systems* (IS) field that focused on the challenges in teaching IS analysis and design. The researcher used an appreciative inquiry modality and utilized experiential learning projects where students were able to apply and reinforce the theories and techniques acquired.

Rytter et al. (2007) carried out an action research study in *operation management* in a Danish company as a part of the development and implementation of new operations strategy. Another study conducted by Näslund et al. (2010) in the *supply chain management* field, used an action research framework to prepare and conduct action research projects. The study advanced a comprehensive action research approach as the foundation of an implementation framework. Finally, Hildrum et al. (2009) describe a study in *R&D and innovation* that was carried out in Norway. The action research was used to facilitate innovation-oriented collaboration between regional industry, R&D and public institutions. The Program for Regional Innovation and R&D established collaboration between a wide variety of actors and served as a catalyst for regional development.

Table 5.2 provides a synopsis of the selected studies briefly captured above. The examples reviewed above illustrate the utilization of action research in a wide variety of business functions or disciplines, and national and regional contexts.

Like the examples of action research in the wide variety of business sectors described earlier, the examples in this section demonstrate the various theoretical foundations that were used and the various and varied content agendas or purposes for the efforts. The common denominators reflected in the studies seem to centre on the emphasis of the orientation of 'study with' versus 'study on', the collaborative nature of action research and the drive to generate scientific knowledge and system improvements. All the studies utilize between four and eight predetermined phases, the cyclical notion of the action research process, and a tapestry of learning mechanisms.

Insider Action Research

As we introduced earlier, it is increasingly common for action research to be conducted from within organizations. In these cases the researchers are managers, at whatever level, who undertake action research on a pressing issue within their own organizations, often as part of their organizational role. There is a growing literature on such experiences and we present three such examples. In the context of the automotive industry facing increasing social pressure to 'go green', Williander and Styhre (2007) reported on an action research study within Volvo Car Corporation that facilitated the process and resulted in some breakthrough innovations. This paper presented the account of an insider action researcher, aimed at studying the development of environmental strategies and 'eco-benign' automobiles 'from the inside'. Similarly, an insider action research mechanism was utilized at AstraZeneca. In this *biopharma* British–Swedish multinational pharmaceutical and biologics company in the UK, three longitudinal action research projects were carried out. Roth et al. (2007) captured and examined the new organizational capabilities that were the outcomes of the project.

Coughlan and Fergus (2009) conducted a two-year action research study in a *manufacturing* company and integrated three paradigms of manufacturing strategy, namely competing through manufacturing, strategic choices in manufacturing, and best practice. The researchers followed three action research cycles over a two-year period. Each cycle comprised a pre-step and four basic steps – diagnosing, planning action, taking action, and evaluating action – and unfolded in real time and began with an understanding of the context of the initiative. When the first cycle was complete, the next cycle began the spiral of steps again. Roth et al. (2004) describe an action research study that focused on the enhancement of an improvement programme within a product development unit in an international telecommunications equipment supplier. Utilizing two cycles of action research, the insider action researcher ran a series of workshops involving functional managers, project managers and process developers to generate a shared interpretation of the data that was collected.

Table 5.2 Examples of action research within business disciplines: Brief synopsis

Business function	Authors, year	Purpose	Key concepts	Outcomes
Customer service	Ballantyne, 2004	Action research in one of four major retail banks in Australia with focus on customer service improvements	Five phases and four steps Knowledge renewal Market-oriented action research	The iterative process of action and learning achieved significant improvements in customer service
E-commerce	Daniel and Wilson, 2004	Action research in eight UK organizations that focused on development methods for prioritization of e-commerce projects	Four phases of action research Two cycles of methods development and experimental implementation	The utilization of the new methods and prioritization matrix achieved a roadmap for action
Finance	Waddell, 2012	Action research project to initiate change by building on a Global Finance Initiative (GFI) of a large global system	Eight-step action research process The integration of three mapping methodologies: visual diagnosis, mind-mapping and social network analysis	The utilization of the eight-step model with three mapping methodologies improved system performance
Human resource	Lindgren et al., 2004	Action research project to develop and test design principles for competence management systems. Six Swedish organizations participated in the project	Two action research cycles New typology of management competence	This research develops an integrative model of HR competence A new typology of competence: competence-in-stock; competence-in-use; competence-in-the-making
IS/IT	Avital, 2005	Appreciative inquiry project to address the challenges in teaching IS analysis and design. Workshops in semester-long course in IS analysis and design	4D cycle (Discovery, Dream, Design and Destiny) Collaborative work design Collaborative participation	Participants gained a formal theory, critical thinking and hands-on experience New skill set in collaborative work

Business function	Authors, year	Purpose	Key concepts	Outcomes
Management, lean management and strategic management	Wyton and Payne, 2014	Action learning project that focused on the way in which action learning groups (ALGs) supported the development of lean capabilities in the facilities management (FM) function of a large organization	A series of 10 two-day workshops Qualitative and quantitative methods Reflective discussions and critical reflective practices	ALGs have an impact on performance Lean can be applied in Facility Management context with the support and contributions by ALGs ALG enhanced new capability development The study led to the development of new ways of working
Manufacturing, operation management (POM) and supply chain management	Rytter et al., 2007	Action research study conducted with a Danish company to generate new operation strategy knowledge	Co-generation and testing of new operation strategy model via action research cycle	New operation strategy model as a tool for describing and analysing real-time operations strategy processes unfolding in practice
	Näslund et al., 2010	Action research study focused on purchasing and supply chain management	Action research cycle based on design aspects, data collection aspects and data analysis aspects	Comprehensive action research framework for guiding action research efforts in the purchasing and supply chain management field
Marketing and e-marketing	Wilson, 2004	Action research study in South Africa to improve marketing planning practice	Action research cycle	Comprehensive framework for conducting action research in the field Improvement of marketing planning practices
R&D and innovation	Hildrum et al., 2009	Action research study to examine the impact of an R&D national programme in Norway	Action research cycle with participation of wide variety of stakeholders in study teams	Comprehensive understanding of the impact of the national R&D programme on regional development

New insights about ways to improve and an improvement programme, new routines for planning and monitoring the progress of improvement projects and new insights into the dual role of insider action research were generated. Table 5.3 provides a synopsis of the selected studies briefly captured above.

Table 5.3   Examples of insider action research: Brief synopsis

Authors, year	Purpose	Key features	Findings
Coughlan and Fergus, 2009	An action research study devoted to exploiting opportunities for superior customer value at lower producer cost	Three cycles of action research over a two-year period	New integrative framework composed of manufacturing strategy, strategic choice and manufacturing best practices Reduction in producer's cost
Roth et al., 2007	An action research study that focused on new capability development within a biopharma company	Four action research cycles Learning mechanisms and processes Insider action research roles and challenges	New insights about the role and challenges of insider action research A tapestry of learning mechanisms as new organizational capability
Roth et al., 2004	An action research study that focused on the enhancement of an improvement programme in a product development unit within an international telecommunications equipment supplier	Two cycles of action research	New insights about ways to improve and an improvement programme New routines for planning and monitoring the progress of improvement projects New insights into the dual role of the insider action researcher
Williander and Styhre, 2007	An action research study devoted to the development of environmental strategies and eco-benign automobiles	Three action research cycles Steering committee and three study teams Designing collaborative research experiments	Insights about the critical role of the insider action researcher New technological inventions Facilitation of new managerial practices and roles

Table 5.4 Examples of action research modalities: Brief synopsis

Dominant action research modality	Authors, year	Purpose	Key features	Findings
Cooperative Inquiry (CI)	Guha et al., 2013	COI study to develop technology design capability and creativity within technical services	CI process to explore phases and process for partnering and co-designing	Wide adoption of CI orientation and practices for software design
			Utilization of co-design methods and technology	Development of design methodology within CI that includes all steps necessary to conceive, develop and produce a technology from start to finish
			Implementation of intergenerational study teams	
Action Learning (AL)	Wyton and Payne, 2014	Action learning study to enhance and support the introduction of lean management capability and practices in a UK company	Ten two-day workshops that included 96 leaders focused on the introduction of the principles, processes and anticipated benefits	The action learning groups provided the processes and learning opportunity to continuously modify and improve lean practices
			Action learning groups were created	Individuals learn lean skill sets to guide practice
			ALGs met regularly to review learning, progress and future tasks	Significant improvements in performance of individuals, teams and areas were recorded
Intervention Research (IR)	Radaelli et al., 2014	IR study to enhance creativity in an Italian fashion design company	Two cycles of IR were implemented	Creativity occurs at a collective level within the organization
			Research team composed of three academics, and three practitioners guided and led the study using collaborative research process design	Implementation of new team design criteria to enhance collective practices
				Institutionalization of learning mechanism tapestry as a new organizational capability

(Continued)

Table 5.4 (Continued)

Dominant action research modality	Authors, year	Purpose	Key features	Findings
Clinical Inquiry Research (CIR)	Stebbins and Shani, 2009	CIR study to design and lead a change initiative aimed at reducing cycle time and costs	CIR process with five phases Research design steering committee was created Six task forces to study specific issues were established	Alternative organization designs were investigated and optimal design proposed Transition process was developed and adopted for implementation The added value from combining CIT, reflective design and collaborative management research was articulated
Collaborative Management Research (CMR)	Canterino et al, 2016	CMR study that focused on the merger process of two real estate investment companies	Two and a half action research cycles were implemented Research team of four academics and four practitioners led and guided the project	CMR can enhance and accelerate the mergers and acquisitions process CMR can generate insights about emerging merger issues and advance specific solutions Learning mechanism can serve as an organizational transformation engine
Appreciative Inquiry (AI)	Thatchenkery and Chowdhry, 2007	AI study to improve knowledge sharing within a bank following series of mergers and acquisitions	The 4-D Cycle of AI (Discovery, Dream, Design and Destiny) was applied Eight sequential AI steps were followed An AI organization summit was designed and managed A tapestry of learning was created	Knowledge enablers were identified Explorations of knowledge sharing mechanisms were investigated Knowledge management system was created

MODALITIES

In Chapter 2 we noted that action research does not constitute a single approach and that it is expressed through different modalities, such as action learning, cooperative inquiry, intervention research, collaborative management research, clinical inquiry research, and appreciative inquiry. In this section we provide some illustrative examples of the framing of action research in terms of some of these modalities. Table 5.4 summarizes these examples.

Guha et al. (2013) reported on a study within the *business and information (tech sector)* industry that used a *cooperative inquiry* methodology. The study demonstrated the utilization of cooperative inquiry in supporting the co-design of experiences with children and clarified seven assumptions about designed partnering with children. Canterino et al. (2016) captured the nature and outcome of a collaborative management research effort that centred on a complex organizational change – the merger process of two real estate investment companies.

Wyton and Payne (2014) used action learning to study the way in which action learning groups supported the development of lean capabilities in the facilities management function of a large organization. In the fashion design industry, an *intervention research* based project with an Italian company was reported by Radaelli et al. (2014). The study focused on creativity and demonstrated how intervention research in the fashion and design industry can be rigorous and relevant to practitioners. Stebbins and Shani (2009) report on a study in the defence industry that utilized a hybrid of *clinical inquiry*, *participative action research* and *collaborative research methodologies*. The study focused on organization redesign within a high technology, secrecy-based company. Last, in the financial and banking industry, an *appreciative inquiry* based project was reported by Thatchenkery and Chowdhry (2007) that focused on the development of a knowledge-sharing system that was needed as a result of a series of mergers and acquisitions.

SUMMARY

In this chapter we have provided a selection of published action research studies to demonstrate the breadth of work across the range of sectors, business functions/disciplines and modalities. As well as demonstrating the wide range across industries and business functions/disciplines, the selection shows the practical nature of the issues addressed and the contribution to knowledge generated through the various actions.

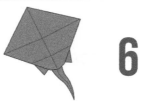

6

CONCLUSIONS

INTRODUCTION

In this chapter we draw together the themes of the preceding five chapters and encapsulate the strengths and limitations of action research, under what conditions it works or does not work, what its contribution is, and we point to how your dissertation might be successful. In Chapter 1 we introduced the complete theory of action research in terms of four factors: i) how you show your understanding of the context in which the action research is taking place, ii) the quality of the collaborative relationship in addressing the issue from the context and in inquiring into its content, process and underlying assumptions, iii) the quality of engaging in cycles of planning action, taking action, reviewing action and articulating learning, and iv) the outcomes of organizational change and developed knowledge. In Chapter 1 we located action research in the history of the tension between knowledge and practice. We introduced the sociotechnical systems, design thinking and organization development as the three conceptual pillars of action research and the different action research modalities. In Chapters 2 and 3 we elaborated these foundational characteristics.

Chapter 4 captured seven activities as specific guidelines and criteria to enhance the overall quality of your action research project as rigorous, reflective and relevant. In our view, while all dissertations are subject to individual examination, these seven activities provide a general framework to support the foundations of a solid (and successful) action research dissertation. Here you might also revisit Eden and Huxham's (1996) 12 contentions in Table 3.1 in Chapter 3 and assess your action research dissertation work across the *core* and *dissertation* projects in terms of their contentions. Chapter 5 provides a wide variety of action research project examples in diverse industries, business disciplines and modalities. The breadth, the wide spread and the added value to practice and theory development of action research since its origin continue to inspire us and we hope that they do the same for you.

WHEN IS ACTION RESEARCH APPROPRIATE?

In what circumstances is action research appropriate? Ronald Lippitt (2016), one of Kurt Lewin's close associates, wrote that the most sophisticated meaning of action research is the situation where participants in a social system, such as an organization, are involved in a data collection process about themselves and they utilize that data to develop new understanding and take some remedial or developmental action. The fields of sociotechnical systems and design thinking advocate the perspective that every system can benefit from the collaborative process in addressing challenges and opportunities. Pendleton-Jullian and Brown (2016) note how triggering pragmatic imagination through systemic action, shared data sense making, shared reflection and thinking is one of the challenges that most systems face.

The cases of Kevin and Talia provide rich examples of how action research was appropriate in their respective contexts and setting. In both case examples, systemic action, collaborative research orientation and design thinking enhanced system improvements and generated new theoretical insights. Action research, as we have seen in this book, is a systematic collaborative discovery process through the implementation of rigorous processes and methods. The action research process creates a context within which the bits and pieces of knowledge that reside with the individual and the social system are surfaced, the knowledge is synthesized through creating a collective understanding and meaning-making process and through a dialogical process that serves as a platform for action.

The nature of social systems and their evolution suggest that staying competitive over time is a challenge. Most organizations rely on their human capital to make the organization work and to stay successful. In most systems, resources are limited, and as such individuals are expected to increasingly do more with less. While knowledge seems to reside within organizational boundaries, due to the nature of the increased work intensity, organizational members share only a limited amount of the knowledge that they hold. As we show across the chapters of this book, action research provides a process and a platform that can enhance information sharing, trigger pragmatic imagination, and inform action and experimentation, knowledge sharing and critical new knowledge creation.

As we have been describing, action research involves engaging on a real issue, while the desire to gather and utilize data in taking action may be more espoused than actual; in other words, if the going gets tough management may get cold feet and withdraw; some initial readiness to embark is essential. Not only is some readiness required but also some capability. Action research is likely to face challenges where there is little or no readiness or capability to engage in a collaborative discovery and reflective process. In settings that are highly politicized, where power is used to control and there is little trust, creating and working with a climate that depends on reflective collaboration, action research may not be feasible.

STRENGTHS AND LIMITATIONS OF ACTION RESEARCH

All research has limitations. Even research that purports to create universal knowledge is limited in what the research question includes and excludes, how data are gathered and how practice is excluded. Given such limitations of all forms of inquiry, we reflect briefly on what we see as the strengths and limitations of action research. The strength of action research is that it contributes to both action and to knowledge. As we discussed in Chapter 1, there is a great deal of debate about the relevance of much management and organizational research as being irrelevant to the world of the practising manager. Action research combines rigour and relevance so that the outcome of an action research initiative is both useful to practice and meets the rigorous standards of scholars. Because action research is conducted in real-time situations with an organization that seeks to address a relevant issue, it generates knowledge about what really goes on in organizations and provides real cases of organizational change. The 'real' referred to here is that action research engages with the actual politics of change and the successful (or unsuccessful) management of politics is often the enabler of successful change. In the respective words of Van de Ven (2007) and Lawler and Mohrman (2011), it is about doing engaged research that is useful.

The particular limitations of action research come from a perspective that understands that the function of research is to create universal knowledge, that is, knowledge that is so broad that it applies to any situation, and thereby is not useful practically. Susman and Evered (1978) argue that, in using the term 'scientific', there is a need to move away from adopting frameworks from natural sciences in order to engage with the world of practice. They show that skill and mastery, personal experience, cycles of action and reflection, human intentionality and a focus on practical outcomes underpin the 'science' of action research. They propose that action research provides a corrective to the deficiencies of traditional science by being future-oriented, collaborative, agnostic and situational, implying system development and so generating theory grounded in action – hence our emphasis on the philosophy of practical knowing as contrasted with theoretical knowing.

ACTION RESEARCH AS A DYNAMIC PROCESS

We have grounded the engagement in action research in three practices and you need to attend to all three. There are the dynamics of working with others: building collaborative relationships around agreeing what is important, enabling consensus as to what to address and how, taking joint action, working with disagreement and conflict and facilitating shared inquiry and learning, to name a few. These make demands on your skills at listening and cooperating. We have called this area of activity and attention second-person practice and it is primary in achieving the goal of the project. At the same time, you need to be attentive to yourself – what is going on in your feelings and thoughts as you engage with others – opening up some relevant self-learning. This is first-person practice and is captured through your use of a reflective journal. In the mode of Schön's (1983) notion of the reflective practitioner, this is also viewed as an opportunity for you to further refine your reflective practitioner skill set.

As we have seen in the different examples provided throughout the book, regardless of the specific context and challenges, some variation of learning mechanisms and learning mechanism tapestries seems to be an integral part of any action research project. Mapping out the learning mechanisms that evolved within the organization over time and how they work can be a way to begin the exploration of which one of the currently utilized learning mechanisms can also be used for the action research project. Such a front-end effort can also help in making the choice of what other learning mechanisms can be designed and developed.

Our experience suggests that an important element of launching a successful masters dissertation is the ability to identify a 'red-hot' topic and explore its potential added value with members of an organization. The dialogue about the importance of the possible topic for the dissertation is likely to trigger further refinement of the possible focus. Being open to hear people, triggering systemic thinking and pragmatic imagination, and exploring meaning and potential relevance generate front-end commitment to support and mentor the project. Most masters dissertations that we have mentored and/or supervised ended up focusing on a research question that was different from the one that the student initially started with. Being open to the idea that the narrow dissertation focus will emerge through dialogue seems critical.

Action research activities trigger the development of a community of inquiry – a form of a tapestry of learning mechanisms – as a way of engaging in this form of research. As Coghlan and Shani (2008) demonstrate, developing a community of inquiry to support and nurture the action research project is likely to be of great help. The initial dialogue about the possible 'red-hot' topic with members of the organization and members of the academic community lays the foundation for the development of a community of inquiry. Intentional development of such a community is beneficial on many levels. A community that involves both insiders and outsiders can help shape and guide the action research project. It can enhance the quality of the project by ensuring that the seven quality criteria identified in Chapter 4 are addressed; it is likely to support you by providing advice and mentoring that can help overcome challenges that are likely to evolve as the project progresses; it is likely to provide a safe platform for critical reflection; it is likely to provide support and guidance for ongoing experimentations; and it is likely to assure the delivery of relevant action and scientific knowledge.

SUMMARY

At the start of Chapter 1 we introduced action research as a rigorous and reflective approach to studying the resolution of important social or organizational issues together with those who experience these issues directly and where the dual goal is to make that action more effective while simultaneously building up a body of actionable knowledge. Throughout the chapters we have elaborated on this simple notion, providing foundational characteristics, historical context, concrete examples and exercises to enable you to engage with your experience and criteria for ensuring the quality of your action research work. People do action research on issues that matter and your engagement with others in a venture to address a shared concern, deliver a desired outcome and co-generate useful and actionable knowledge is a powerful intervention in any system, organization, community or region and indeed in our world.

GLOSSARY OF TERMS

Action: The action is directed at addressing a real organizational issue, whether a problem to be solved or an opportunity to be exploited.

Action learning: An approach to learning through engaging with a group of peers which provides reflective space, support and challenge to work through a problem.

Action research: A family of related approaches is an emergent inquiry process in which applied behavioural science knowledge is integrated with existing organizational knowledge and applied to address real organizational issues.

Action research components: Action research has four components: action, research, collaboration and reflexivity.

Action Science: Focuses on systemically analysing and documenting patterns of behaviours and the reasoning behind them in order to identify causal links so as to produce actionable knowledge, that is, theories for producing desired outcomes.

Appreciative Inquiry: A form of action research which focuses on building on what is already successful, rather than what is deficient, thus leveraging the generative capacity for transformational action.

Change design framework: A framework that is comprised of six steps: 1) Identify the need for change; 2) Build appropriate collaborative relationships; 3) Frame a desired outcome for the change; 4) Develop a change plan and design the learning mechanisms; 5) Implement the change plan and manage the transition; 6) Reinforce and sustain the change through the learning mechanisms.

Choice points: Places in an inquiry when choices present themselves and need to be addressed in a conscious and transparent manner.

Clinical Inquiry/Research: Action researchers gain access to organizations at the organization's invitation to be helpful and intervene in order to enable change to occur.

Clinical perspective: Questioning and studying events that arouse a researcher's curiosity.

Cognitive learning mechanisms: The bearers of language, concepts, symbols, theories, frameworks, and values for thinking, reasoning, and understanding consistent with the new capabilities.

Collaborative: Action research is collaborative in that it emphasizes research *with* people rather than *on* or *for* them, and so it differentiates action research from traditional research approaches.

Collaborative Developmental Action Inquiry: A form of action science that builds on insights from developmental psychology, especially how leaders can understand their own developmental stages and thereby gain insight into their own action-logics as they work to transform their organizations.

Collaborative Management Research: Here external researchers and members of the system collaborate on the study of an organizational issue through a joint project of deliberate change.

Confrontive inquiry: Here a researcher shares their own ideas and challenges their co-inquirers to think from an alternative perspective.

Content reflection: Reflecting on what is done or discussed.

Cooperative Inquiry: Here participants research a topic through their own experience of it in order to understand their world, to make sense of their life and develop new and creative ways of looking at things and learn how to act to change things they might want to change and find out how to do things better.

Core project: This is the action project on which researchers in an action research project are working within the organization.

Cycles of action and reflection: How action influences reflection and reflection influences action.

Design thinking: A human-centred framework aimed at creative problem solving with the intent to foster creativity and innovation. It employs divergent thinking as a way to ensure that a wide variety of solutions are explored and convergent thinking is utilized to narrow down these toward a specific solution.

Diagnostic inquiry: Inquiry in which a researcher begins to guide co-inquirers' thinking process by asking questions that elicit their causal thinking. A form of second-person practice.

Dialogic: Understanding that organizations comprise multiple perspectives and meanings, rather than one technical reality. This leads to an emphasis on changing the conversation by surfacing, legitimating and learning from multiple perspectives and generating new images and narratives on which people can act.

Dissertation action research project: This project involves inquiry into the core project and makes a contribution to the academic literature.

Emergent theory: The theory that develops from a synthesis of the understanding which emerges from reflection on the project data and from the use in practice of the body of relevant theories which informed the research purpose.

Engaged scholarship: An approach to scholarship that combines rigour and relevance. Conducted in real-time situations with an organization that seeks to address a relevant issue, it generates knowledge about what really goes on in organizations and provides cases of real organizational change.

First-person practice: Attending to one's own thinking, valuing, way of learning and behaving.

General empirical method: A method based on the recognizable and invariant process of human knowing.

Inquiry: Asking questions and seeking answers. Often a less formal or threatening word than research.

Insider action research: Conducting action research in the organization or community in which one is employed or a member.

Intervention: Doing or saying something that alters the status quo.

Intervention Research: A detailed analysis of an organization's performance and the consequent development of management tools and actions to address deeply embedded problems.

Journaling: Keeping a reflective notebook that captures both events of the project and one's own thoughts and feelings about the events and one's own learning in action.

Learning mechanism: Planned organizational structures and processes that encourage dynamic learning, particularly to enhance or create new organizational capabilities.

Meta cycle: Cycle of action and reflection about the cycles of action and reflection.

Meta-learning: Learning about learning.

Methodology: The overarching theory of the methods used.

Methods: Techniques and tools for designing and implementing the research.

Mode 1 knowledge production: Research that arises from the academic agenda and is conducted within a singular discipline and is accountable to that discipline.

Mode 2 knowledge production: Combines theoretical knowledge with applied, practical knowledge to solve particular scientific and organizational problems.

Narrative: The story of what took place: cycles of action and reflection as a systematic method in planning action, taking action, reviewing outcomes and process and generating understanding.

Organization development: An approach to organizational change based on action research that is a philosophy, a professional field of social action, a mode of scientific inquiry and an array of techniques to enable change to take place in organizations.

Practical knowing: Knowing how to take action.

Pragmatic imagination: A framework that sees the imagination as a spectrum of coherent process that moves between data sense-making and sense breaking.

Premise reflection: Critiquing taken-for-granted assumptions and perspectives.

Preunderstanding: The knowledge that a researcher brings to the research project.

Procedural learning mechanisms: The rules, routines, methods and tools that can be institutionalized in the organization to promote and support learning.

Process reflection: Reflecting on how things are done.

Pure inquiry: Researchers listening carefully to others' accounts of their experience of the issues at hand and eliciting and exploring their story of what is taking place.

Quality: Meeting the requirements of good quality action research.

Reflection: A process of standing back from experience to question it and to have insights. It involves not simply describing experience but also doing some analysis through exploring links between behaviour and outcomes, questioning ideas and assumptions seeking understanding.

Reflective practitioner: A practitioner (an action researcher or an employee or a manager) that developed the skill set to both reflect-on-action and reflect-in-action.

Reflexive: Action research is *reflexive* in that by taking place in the present tense it requires a constant examination and evaluation of what is going on with a view to deciding what needs to happen next.

Research: The scientific discovery process, which contributes to practical knowing.

Roles: Patterns of behaviour which individuals expect of others performing specific functions or tasks.

Second-person practice: This addresses engagement in collaborative work in co-inquiry and shared action with others on issues of mutual concern, through face-to-face dialogue, conversation and joint action.

Sociotechnical system: A comprehensive organization and management school of thought that views an organization as an entity composed of three subsystems:

environmental, technical and social. The organizations comprise of a social system (the people) and a technical system (tasks and technology) that function within a specific environmental context.

Structural learning mechanisms: Organizational, physical, technical and work system infrastructures that encourage practice-based learning.

Third-person practice: Extending first- and second-person learning to an impersonal audience, those who were not directly involved in the project. This includes dissemination through reporting, publishing and being examined.

REFERENCES

Adler, N. and Docherty, P. (1998) Bringing business into sociotechnical theory and practice. *Human Relations*, 51(3): 319-345.

Argyris, C. and Schön, D.A. (1974) *Theory in Practice: Increasing Professional Effectiveness*. San Francisco: Jossey-Bass.

Argyris, C., Putnam, R. and Smith, D. (1985) *Action Science*. San Francisco: Jossey-Bass.

Aristotle (1961) *Metaphysics* (Vol. 1, Bks. 1-9; Vol. 2, Bks. 10-14), H. Tredennick, trans. Cambridge, MA: Harvard University Press.

Avital, M. (2005) Innovation information systems education I: Accelerated systems analysis and design with appreciative inquiry – an action learning approach. *Communications of the Association for Information Systems*, 15: 289-314.

Baker, T. and Jayaraman, V. (2012) Managing information and supplies inventory operations in a manufacturing environment, Part 1: An action research study. *International Journal of Production Research*, 50(6): 1666-1681.

Ballantyne, D. (2004) Action research reviewed: A market-oriented approach. *European Journal of Marketing*, 38(3/4): 321-337.

Bartunek, J.M. (1983) How organization development can develop organization theory. *Group & Organization Management*, 8(3): 303-318.

Basset, S. (2013) *The Reflective Journal*. London: Palgrave.

Beckhard, R. and Harris, R. (1987) *Organizational Transitions: Managing Complex Change*, 2nd edn. Reading, MA: Addison-Wesley.

Blumberg, M. and Pringle, C.D. (1983) How control groups can cause loss of control in action research: The case of Rushton Coal Mine. *The Journal of Applied Behavioral Science*, 19(4): 409-425.

Bradbury, H., Roth, G. and Gearty, M.R. (2015) The practice of learning history. In H. Bradbury (ed.), *The SAGE Handbook of Action Research*, 3rd edn. London: Sage. pp. 17-30.

Brown, T. (2008) Design thinking. *Harvard Business Review*, 86, June: 84-92.

Buchanan, D. and Badham, R. (2008) *Power, Politics, and Organizational Change: Winning the Turf Game*, 2nd edn. London: Sage.

Burnes, B. (2007) Kurt Lewin and the Harwood studies: The foundations of OD. *Journal of Applied Behavioral Science*, 43(2): 213-231.

Bushe, G. and Marshak, R. (2015) *Dialogic Organization Development: The Theory and Practice of Transformational Change.* San Francisco: Berrett-Kohler.

Canterino, F., Shani, A.B. (Rami), Coghlan, D. and Bruneli, M. (2016) Collaborative management research as a modality of action research: Learning from a merger-based study. *Journal of Applied Behavioral Science*, 52(2): 157-186.

Cassell, C. (2015) *Conducting Research Interviews.* London: Sage.

Chandler, D. and Torbert, W.R. (2003) Transforming inquiry and action: Interweaving 27 flavors of action research. *Action Research*, 1(2): 133-152.

Coch, L. and French, J. (1948) Overcoming resistance to change. *Human Relations*, 1: 512-533.

Coghlan, D. (2001) Insider action research projects: Implications for practising managers. *Management Learning*, 32: 49-60.

Coghlan, D. (2009) Toward a philosophy of clinical inquiry/research. *Journal of Applied Behavioral Science*, 45(1): 106-121.

Coghlan, D. (2011) Action research: Exploring perspective on a philosophy of practical knowing. *Academy of Management Annals*, 5: 53-87.

Coghlan, D. (2015) Organization development: Action research for organizational change. In H. Bradbury (ed.), *The SAGE Handbook of Action Research*, 3rd edn. London: Sage. pp. 417-424.

Coghlan, D. (2016) Retrieving the philosophy of practical knowing for action research. *International Journal of Action Research*, 12(1): 84-107.

Coghlan, D. and Brannick, T. (2014) *Doing Action Research in Your Own Organisation*, 4th edn. London: Sage.

Coghlan, D. and Brydon-Miller, M. (eds) (2014). *The SAGE Encyclopedia of Action Research.* 2 volumes. London: Sage.

Coghlan, D. and Shani, A.B. (Rami) (2005) Roles, politics and ethics in action research design. *Systemic Practice and Action Research*, 18(6): 533-546.

Coghlan, D. and Shani, A.B. (Rami) (2008) Collaborative management research through communities of inquiry. In A.B. (Rami) Shani, S.A. Mohrman, W.A. Pasmore, B. Stymne and N. Adler (eds), *Handbook of Collaborative Management Research.* London: Sage. pp. 601-614.

Coghlan, D. and Shani, A.B. (Rami) (eds) (2016) *Action Research in Business and Management.* 4 volumes. London: Sage.

Coghlan, D. and Shani, A.B. (Rami) (2017) Inquiring in the present tense: The dynamic mechanism of action research. *Journal of Change Management*, 17(2): 121-137.

Coghlan, D., Rashford, N.S. and Neiva de Figueiredo, J. (2016) *Organizational Change and Strategy: An Interlevels Dynamics Approach*, 2nd edn. Abingdon: Routledge.

Coughlan, P. and Fergus, M.A. (2009) Defining the path to value innovation. *International Journal of Manufacturing Technology and Management*, 16(3): 234-249.

Cronin, B. (2017) *Phenomenology of Human Understanding*. Eugene, OR: Pickwick Publications.

Cummings, T.G. (1980) *Systems Theory for Organizational Development*. Somerset, NJ: John Wiley & Sons.

Daniel, E. and Wilson, H.N. (2004) Action research in turbulent environments: An example in e-commerce prioritization. *European Journal of Marketing*, 38(3/4): 355-377.

David, A. and Hatchuel, A. (2008) From actionable knowledge to universal theory in management research. In A.B. (Rami) Shani, S.A. Mohrman, W.A. Pasmore, B. Stymne and N. Adler, *Handbook of Collaborative Management Research*. Thousand Oaks, CA: Sage. pp. 33-47.

Dewey, J. (1933) *How We Think*. New York: Heath.

Dunne, J. (1993) *Back to the Rough Ground: 'Phronesis' and 'Techne' in Modern Philosophy and in Aristotle* . South Bend, IN: University of Notre Dame Press.

Eden, C. and Huxham, C. (1996) Researching organizations using action research. *British Journal of Management*, 7(1): 75-86. Reproduced in D. Coghlan and A.B. (Rami) Shani (eds) (2016), *Action Research in Business and Management*, Vol. I. London: Sage. pp. 261-278.

Emery, E. (1959) *Characteristics of Sociotechnical Systems*. London: Tavistock Institute.

Gibbons, M., Limoges, C., Nowotny, H., Schwartzman, S., Scott, P. and Trow, M. (1994) *The New Production of Knowledge*. London: Sage.

Guha, M.L., Druin, A. and Failsb, J.A. (2013) Cooperative inquiry revisited: Reflections of the past and guidelines for the future of intergenerational co-design. *International Journal of Child-Computer Interaction*, 1: 14-23.

Gummesson, E. (2000) *Qualitative Methods in Management Research*, 2nd edn. Thousand Oaks, CA: Sage.

Hanna, D. (1988) *Designing Organizations for High Performance*. Reading, MA: Addison-Wesley.

Heron, J. (1996) *Co-operative Inquiry*. London: Sage.

Heron, J. and Reason, P. (1997) A participatory inquiry paradigm. *Qualitative Inquiry*, 3: 274-294.

Hildrum, J.D., Finsrud, H.D. and Klethagen, P. (2009) The next generation of national R&D programmes in Norway: Consequences for action research and regional development. *International Journal of Action Research*, 5(3): 255-288.

Kahneman, D. (2011) *Thinking, fast and slow*. New York: Penguin.

King, N. and Brookes, J.M. (2017) *Template Analysis for Business and Management Students*. London: Sage.

Kleiner, A. and Roth, G. (1997) How to make experience your company's best teacher. *Harvard Business Review*, September-October: 172-177.

Kocher, P., Kaudela-Baum, S. and Wolf, P. (2011) Enhancing organizational innovation capability through systemic action research: A case of a Swiss SME in the food industry. *Systemic Practice & Action Research*, 24(1): 17-44.

Kotter, J.P. (1995) Leading change: Why transformation efforts fail. *Harvard Business Review*, March–April: 59–67.

Lawler, E.E. and Mohrman, S.A (2011) *Useful Research: Advancing Theory and Practice*. San Francisco: Berrett-Koehler.

Levin, M. and Greenwood, D. (2016) *Creating a New Public University and Reviving Democracy: Action Research in Higher Education*. New York: Berghahn.

Lewin, K. (1997) Action research and minority problems. In K. Lewin, *Resolving Social Conflicts*. Washington, DC: American Psychological Association. pp. 143–154. (Original publication 1946.)

Lewin, K. (2016) The solution of a chronic problem in industry. In D. Coghlan and A.B. (Rami) Shani (eds), Action Research in Business and Management, Vol. 1. London: Sage. pp. 3–16. (Original publication 1944.)

Lillrank, P., Shani, A.B. (Rami) and Lindberg, P. (2001) Continuous improvement: Exploring alternative designs. *Total Quality Management*, 12(1): 41–55.

Lindgren, R., Henfridsson, O. and Schultze, U. (2004) Design principles for competence management systems: A synthesis of an action research study. *MIS Quarterly*, 28(3): 435–472.

Lippitt, R. (2016) Kurt Lewin, action research and planned change. In D. Coghlan and A.B. (Rami) Shani (eds), *Action Research in Business and Management*, Vol. I. London: Sage. pp. 23–27.

Lipshitz, R., Popper, M. and Friedman, V.J. (2002) A multifaceted model of organizational learning. *Journal of Applied Behavioral Science*, 38: 78–98.

Ludema, J. and Fry, R. (2008) The practice of appreciative inquiry. In P. Reason and H. Bradbury (eds), *The SAGE Handbook of Action Research*, 2nd edn. London: Sage. pp. 280–296.

Lund, A.B. (2008) Diffusion of innovations in news organizations: Action research of middle managers in Danish mass media. In C. Dal Zotto and H. van Kranenburg (eds), *Management and Innovation in the Media Industry*. Cheltenham: Edward Elgar. pp. 199–214.

McKay, J. and Marshall, P. (2001) The dual imperatives of action research. *Information Technology & People*, 14(1): 46–59.

MacLean, D., McIntosh, R. and Grant, S. (2002) Model 2 management research. *British Journal of Management*, 13(2): 189–207.

Marshall, J. (2016) *First Person Action Research: Living Life as Inquiry*. London: Sage.

Martin, R. (2009) The Design of Business: Why Design Thinking is the Next Competitive Advantage. Boston, MA: Harvard Business Press.

Meister, D.B. and Gronski, C.M. (2007) Action research in a virtual setting: Cautions from a failed project. In N. Koch (ed.), *Information Systems Action Research*. New York: Springer. pp. 217–239.

Miller, J.H. and Page, S.E. (2007) *Complex Adaptive Systems*. Princeton, NJ: Princeton University Press.

Mitki, Y., Shani, A.B. (Rami) and Stjernberg, T. (2000) A typology of change programs and their differences from a solid perspective. In R.T. Golembiewski (ed.), *Handbook of Organizational Consultation*, 2nd edn. New York: Marcel Dekker Inc. pp. 777–785.

Mitki, Y., Shani, A.B. (Rami) and Stjernberg, T. (2008) Leadership, development and learning mechanisms: Systems transformation as a balancing act. *Journal of Organizational Change Management*, 29(1): 68–84.

Mohrman, S. and Shani, A.B. (Rami) (2011) Organizing for sustainable effectiveness: Taking stock and moving forward. In S. Mohrman and A.B. (Rami) Shani, *Organizing for Sustainability*. Bingley, UK: Emerald. pp. 1–40.

Moon, J. (1999) *Learning Journals*. London: Kogan Page.

Näslund, D., Kale, R. and Paulraj, A. (2010) Action research in supply chain management: A framework for relevant and rigorous research. *Journal of Business Logistics*, 31(2): 331–355.

Neilsen, E. (2006) But let us not forget John Collier. *Action Research*, 4(4): 389–400.

Ngwerume, K.T. and Themessl-Huber, M. (2010) Using action research to develop a research aware community pharmacy team. *Action Research*, 8(4): 387–406.

Nowotny, H., Scott, P. and Gibbons, M. (2001) *Rethinking Science: Knowledge and the Public in an Age of Uncertainty*. London: Polity Press.

Pace, L.A. and Argona, D.R. (1989) Participative action research: A view from Xerox. *American Behavioral Scientist*, 32(5): 552–565.

Parry, R. (2003) *Episteme* and *techne*. In E.N. Zalta (ed.), *The Stanford Encyclopedia of Philosophy*. Retrieved from https://plato.stanford.edu/entries/episteme-techne/ (Accessed 18th May 2018).

Pasmore, W.A. (1988) *Designing Effective Organizations: The Sociotechnical Systems Perspective*. New York, NY: Wiley.

Pasmore, W.A. (1994) *Creating Strategic Change: Designing the Flexible High-Performing Organizations*. New York: John Wiley & Sons.

Pasmore, W.A. (2001) Action research in the workplace: The socio-technical perspective. In P. Reason and H. Bradbury (eds), *Handbook of Action Research*. London: Sage. pp. 38–47.

Pasmore, W.A. (2011) Tipping the balance: Overcoming persistent problems in organizational change. In A.B. (Rami) Shani, R.W. Woodman and W.A. Pasmore (eds), *Research in Organizational Change and Development*, Vol. 19. Bingley, UK: Emerald. pp. 259–292.

Pasmore, W.A., Woodman, R. and Simmons, A.L. (2008) Toward a more rigorous, reflective, and relevant science of collaborative management research. In A.B. (Rami) Shani, S. Mohrman, W.A. Pasmore, B. Stymne and N. Adler (eds), *Handbook of Collaborative Management Research*. Thousand Oaks, CA: Sage. pp. 567–582.

Pavlovsky, P., Forslin, J. and Reinhart, R. (2001) Practices and tools of organizational learning. In M. Dierkes, A. Berthoin Antal, J. Child and I. Nonaka (eds), *Handbook of Organizational Learning and Knowledge*. Oxford: Oxford University Press. pp. 775–793.

Pedler, M. and Burgoyne, J.G. (2015) Action learning. In H. Bradbury (ed.), *The SAGE Handbook of Action Research*, 3rd edn. London: Sage. pp. 179-187.

Pendleton-Jullian, A. and Brown, J.S. (2016) *Pragmatic Imagination*. CPSIA Publication. Available at: www.ICGtesting.com.

Radaelli, G., Guerci, M., Cirella, S. and Shani, A.B. (Rami) (2014) Intervention research as management research in practice: Learning from a case in the fashion design industry. *British Journal of Management*, 25: 335-351.

Reason, P. (2006) Choice and quality in action research practice. *Journal of Management Inquiry*, 15: 187-203.

Roth, J., Sandberg, R. and Svensson, C. (2004) The dual role of the insider action researcher. In N. Adler, A.B. (Rami) Shani and B. Stymne (eds), *Collaborative Research in Organizations*. Thousand Oaks, CA: Sage. pp. 117-134.

Roth, J., Shani, A.B. (Rami) and Leary, M. (2007) Insider action research: Facing the challenge of new capability development. *Action Research*, 5: 41-60.

Rytter, N.G., Boer, H. and Koch, C. (2007) Conceptualizing operations strategy processes. *International Journal of Operations & Production Management*, 27(10): 1093-1114.

Saunders, M., Dietz, G. and Thornhill, A. (2014) Trust and distrust: Polar opposites, or independent but co-existing? *Human Relations*, 67: 639-665.

Savall, H. and Zardet, V. (2011) *The Qualimetrics Approach*. Charlotte, NC: Information Age Publishing.

Schein, E.H. (2008) Clinical inquiry/research. In P. Reason and H. Bradbury (eds), *The SAGE Handbook of Action Research*, 2nd edn. London: Sage. pp. 266-279.

Schein, E.H. (2009) *Helping*. San Francisco: Berrett-Koehler.

Schein, E.H. (2010) Organization development: Science, technology or philosophy? In D. Coghlan and A.B. (Rami) Shani, *Fundamentals of Organization Development*, Vol. 1. London: Sage. pp. 91-100.

Schein, E.H. (2013a) Notes toward a model of organizational therapy. In L. Vansina (ed.), *Humanness in Organizations*. London: Karnac. pp. 91-100.

Schein, E.H. (2013b) *Humble Inquiry: The Gentle Art of Asking Instead of Telling*. San Francisco: Berrett-Koehler.

Schein, E.H. and Schein P.A. (2018) *Humble Leadership: The Power of Relationships, Openness, and Trust*. San Francisco: Berrett-Koehler.

Schön, D. (1983) *The Reflective Practitioner: How Professionals Think in Action*. New York, NY: Basic Books.

Shani, A.B. (Rami) and Docherty, P. (2003) *Learning by Design: Building Sustainable Organizations*. Oxford: Blackwell.

Shani, A.B. (Rami) and Eberhardt, B. (1987) Parallel organization in a health care institution: An exploratory action research study. *Group and Organization Studies*, 12(2): 147-173.

Shani, A.B. (Rami) and Elliott, O. (1989) Sociotechnical system design in transition. In W. Sikes, A. Drexler and J. Grant (eds), *The Emerging Practice of Organization Development*. La Jolla, CA: University Associates. pp. 187-198.

Shani, A.B. (Rami) and Pasmore W.A. (2016) Organization inquiry: Towards a new model of the action research process. In D. Coghlan and A.B. (Rami) Shani (eds), *Action Research in Business and Management*, Vol. 1. London: Sage. pp. 191–200. (Original publication 1985.)

Shani, A.B. (Rami), Mohrman, S., Pasmore, W.A., Stymne, B. and Adler, N. (eds) (2008) *Handbook of Collaborative Management Research*. Thousand Oaks, CA: Sage.

Shani, A.B. (Rami), Tenkasi, R.V. and Alexander, B.N. (2017) Knowledge and practice: A historical perspective on collaborative management research. In J. Bartunek and J. McKenzie (eds), *Academic Practitioner Research Partnership: Developments, Complexities and Opportunities*. Abingdon: Routledge. pp. 17–34.

Smith, D.M. (2015) Action science revisited: Building knowledge out of practice to transform practice. In H. Bradbury (ed.), *The SAGE Handbook of Action Research*, 3rd edn. London: Sage. pp. 143–157.

Stebbins, M.W. and Shani, A.B. (Rami) (2009) Clinical inquiry and reflective design in a secrecy-based organization. *The Journal of Applied Behavioral Science*, 45(1): 59–89.

Susman, G.I. and Evered, R.D. (1978) An assessment of the scientific merits of action research. *Administrative Science Quarterly*, 23: 582–601.

Taylor, J.C. and Felten, D.F. (1993) *Performance by Design: Sociotechnical Systems*. Englewood Cliffs, NJ: Prentice Hall.

Tenkasi, R.V. and Hay, G.W. (2008) Following the second legacy of Aristotle: The scholar-practitioner as an epistemic-technician. In A.B. (Rami) Shani, S.A. Mohrman, W.A. Pasmore, B. Stymne and N. Adler (eds), *Handbook of Collaborative Management Research*. Thousand Oaks, CA: Sage. pp. 49–72.

Thatchenkery, T. and Chowdhry, D. (2007) *Appreciative Inquiry and Knowledge Management*. Cheltenham, UK: Edward Elgar.

Torbert, W.R. (1991) *The Power of Balance*. Thousand Oaks, CA: Sage.

Torbert, W.R. and Associates (2004) *Action Inquiry*. San Francisco: Jossey-Bass.

Trist, E.L. (1982) The evolution of sociotechnical systems. In A. Van de Ven and W.F. Joyce (eds), *Perspectives on Organization Design and Behavior*. New York: John Wiley & Sons. pp. 19–75.

Van de Ven, A. (2007) *Engaged Scholarship*. New York: Oxford University Press.

Van Eijnatten, F.M., Shani, A.B. (Rami) and Leary, M. (2008) Sociotechnical systems: Designing and managing sustainable organizations. In T. Cummings (ed.), *Handbook of Organization Development*. Thousand Oaks, CA: Sage. pp. 277–309.

Waddell, S. (2012) Global finance as an action research domain: Testing the boundaries. *Action Research*, 10(1): 40–60.

Walton, R.E. and Gaffney, M.E. (1989) Research, action and participation: The merchant shipping case. *American Behavioral Scientist*, 32(5): 582–611.

Whitehead, D. (2005) Project management and action research: Two sides of the same coin? *Journal of Health Organization and Management*, 19(6): 519–531.

Williander, M. and Styhre, A. (2007) Going green from the inside: Insider action research at the Volvo Car Corporation. *Systemic Practice and Action Research,* 19: 239–252.

Wilson, H.N. (2004) Towards rigour in action research: A case study in marketing planning. *European Journal of Marketing,* 38(3/4): 378–400.

Wyton, P. and Payne, R. (2014) Exploring the development of competence in lean management through action learning groups: A study of the introduction of lean to a facilities management function. *Action Learning: Research and Practice,* 11(1): 42–61.

Zuber-Skerritt, O. and Perry, C. (2002) Action research within organizations and university thesis writing. *The Learning Organization,* 9: 171–179.

INDEX